BARBECUE

D0102490

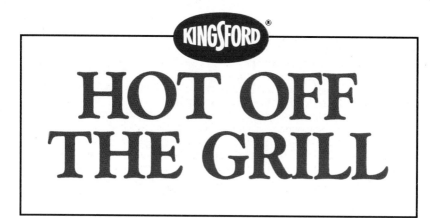

HOT OFF THE GRILL

Ah, barbecue—the mere mention of authentic charcoal cooking conjures up images of sensational food and summer fun. It's a style of cooking that tantalizes our taste buds with its fragrant, mouth-watering aromas, and offers cooks endless opportunities for flavorful experimenting. If you're new to the world of barbecue, we've included all the basics for getting started. And for the experienced outdoor chef, we offer plenty of intriguing menus to keep your grill fired up all summer—and winter—long!

A DASH OF HISTORY

Henry Ford gets credit for more than the Model T. His ingenuity is responsible for launching America's passion for outdoor cooking. You might say he's the original baron of barbecue—all because he couldn't tolerate waste.

In the early 1900s, Ford operated a northern Michigan saw mill that made wooden framing for his Model Ts. He looked on in frustration at the growing piles of wood scraps and wondered how they could be put to productive use. He came up with the idea to chip the wood into small pieces, convert it to charcoal, grind it into powder, then compress it into the now-familiar pillow-shaped briquets. These convenient briquets were originally sold through Ford automobile agencies.

Ford put his brother-in-law, E. G. Kingsford, in charge of the charcoal operation. Together, they helped make barbecuing an American tradition. Ford Charcoal Briquets, later named **Kingsford**®, is the original and still the number one brand sold in the nation today.

TYPES OF CHARCOAL

Successful barbecuing starts with a good fire. Premium quality briquets, like **Kingsford**® charcoal, help deliver a perfect fire three ways. They light quicker so the coals are ready sooner. They burn more evenly to produce balanced heat, and they perform consistently, bag after bag. The renewed interest in authentic charcoal cooking has spawned extra convenience and new flavor in the types of charcoal available.

Instant Lighting Charcoal Briquets. These are an especially good choice for mid-week barbecues when time is at a premium. Products like **Match light®** charcoal briquets already have just the right amount of lighter fluid to produce a quick-starting fire. Simply stack the briquets into a pyramid and light several briquets with a match. The coals are ready in about 20 minutes. Close the bag tightly after each use to prevent evaporation of lighter fluid.

Charcoal Briquets with Mesquite Wood Chips. The perfect selection for cooks who enjoy the wonderful flavor of mesquite but feel less comfortable grilling over pure mesquite charcoal, which burns hotter and less evenly. For example, **Kingsford® with Mesquite** charcoal briquets are compressed charcoal briquets with mesquite chips blended into them. These briquets produce real mesquite smoke to enhance the flavor of outdoor fare.

It's important to remember that charcoal is porous and will absorb moisture. Always store briquets in a dry area, and keep the bag tightly closed or in a covered container. Charcoal that has been exposed to humidity or moisture can be more difficult to light.

SAFETY FIRST

Make sure the grill is on a solid surface and is set away from shrubbery, grass and overhangs. NEVER use gasoline or kerosene as a lighter fluid starter. Either one can cause an explosion. To get a sluggish fire going, *do not add lighter fluid directly to hot coals.* Instead, take 2 to 3 additional briquets, place them in a small metal container and add lighter fluid. When the briquets have absorbed the fuel (1 to 2 minutes), add them to the pyramid of briquets, then light with a match. These briquets will restart the fire.

Remember that coals are hot—up to 1000°F—and that the heat transfers to the barbecue grill, grid, tools and food. Always wear fireproof mitts when cooking and handling grill and tools.

BUILDING PERFECT FIRES

If you're new to the world of barbecue, don't be intimidated about getting started. Follow these steps and discover how easy it is to build a perfect fire.

How much Charcoal? A 5-pound bag of **Kingsford®** charcoal contains 75 to 90 briquets; a 10-pound bag between 150 and 180; and a 20-pound bag 300 to 360 briquets. The number of briquets required for barbecuing depends on the size and type of grill and the amount of food to be prepared. Weather conditions also have an effect; strong winds, very cold temperatures, or highly humid conditions increase the number of briquets needed for a good fire. As a rule of thumb, it takes about 30 briquets to grill 1 pound of meat. For example, you'll need 45 briquets to grill six 4-ounce hamburgers.

For grilling meat directly over the coals, you want enough charcoal—in a single layer—to extend about 1 to 2 inches beyond the area of the food on the grill. Pour enough briquets into the grill unit to determine the quantity needed, then stack them into a pyramid.

Using Lighter Fluid. Stack briquets into a pyramid. Soak briquets with at least ½ cup lighter fluid. Wait 1 minute to allow fluid to soak into briquets. Then light with a match. Coals are ready when they are about 80% ashed over. At night, they will have a noticeable cheery glow. The coals will be ready to use in 20 to 30 minutes.

Using a Chimney Starter. This method is essentially failure-proof and no lighter fluid is required. Here's how to use one. First, remove the grid from the grill and set the chimney starter in the base of the grill. Then crumble a couple of sheets of newspaper and place them in the bottom portion of the chimney starter. Fill top portion with charcoal briquets. Light the newspaper. Do not disturb the starter; coals will be ready in 20 to 30 minutes. Be sure to wear fireproof mitts when emptying coals from the chimney starter into the base of the grill.

Using an Electric Starter. Nestle the electric starter in the coals. Then plug the starter into a heavy-duty extension cord. Plug the cord into the nearest available outlet. After 8 to 10 minutes, when ash begins to form on the briquets, unplug the starter, remove it, and carefully set it aside. Arrange the briquets in a single layer, close together.

When cooking in a covered grill using an indirect method, food is placed over a drip pan and the coals are banked either to one or both sides of the pan. This method is recommended for large cuts of meat (like roasts) and for fatty meats, to eliminate flame flare-ups. Here's how to determine the number of briquets needed:

Briquets Needed for Indirect Cooking, Covered Grill

	Diameter of Grill (inches)			
	26¾	22½	18½	14
Briquets needed each side of drip pan for cooking 45 to 50 minutes	30	25	16	15
Number of briquets to be added on each side of drip pan every 45 minutes	9	8	5	4

How Hot is the Grill? If you don't have a grill thermometer, here is a quick, easy way to estimate the temperature on the grill surface. Hold your hand, palm-side-down, just above the grid. Count "one thousand one, one thousand two," etc., until the heat is uncomfortable. If you can keep your hand in place before pulling away:

- 2 seconds—it's a hot fire, about 375°F or more.
- 3 seconds—it's a medium-hot fire, about 350° to 375°F.
- 4 seconds—it's a medium fire, about 300° to 350°F.
- 5 seconds—it's a low fire, about 200° to 300°F.

BARBECUE TIPS

For best results, bring fish, poultry and meat to room temperature before cooking.

To keep food from sticking to the grid and make it easy to turn, rub the grid with vegetable oil before cooking.

When making kabobs, if you use wooden or bamboo skewers, be sure to soak them in cold water 20 minutes before grilling.

The secret to evenly cooked vegetable and meat kabobs is to parboil solid or starchy vegetables before they are threaded onto skewers for grilling.

Always use tongs or a spatula when handling meat. Piercing meat with a fork allows delicious juices to escape and makes meat less moist.

Basting sauces made with honey, sugar or tomato retain best flavor and color when added during the last 10 minutes of grilling. Baste again just before serving.

Foods wrapped in foil and cooked on the grill should be turned often to prevent burning and assure even cooking.

When barbecuing food for more than 45 minutes, add 10 to 12 briquets around the outer edge of the fire as cooking starts. When these briquets are ready, add them to the center of the fire as needed to maintain constant temperature.

Fish grills quickly and deliciously over a moderately hot fire. To check for doneness, cut into the thickest part with a knife and fork. Fish is ready when it flakes. Shellfish is ready when it turns a milky color and is opaque.

A WORD ABOUT SAUCES

Sauces, rich and thick with tomato, and savory with garlic, onion and spices, add delicious flavor to almost any grilled fare. Premium sauces, like **K.C. Masterpiece®** Barbecue Sauce, capture real homemade taste and are a barbecue staple worth using often. Serve warmed sauce on the side for added zest. Here's how to protect the rich, deep color and spicy flavor of barbecue sauce, especially tomato- and molasses-based ones that can burn if applied too early:

- For Grilled Steaks and Chops: add sauce after meat has been turned for the last time, about the last 3 minutes of grilling.
- For Grilled Chicken: add sauce the last 10 minutes, turn once.
- For Hot Dogs and Sausage: add sauce the last 5 to 6 minutes.
- For Barbecued Meats (cooked by indirect method): add sauce the last hour of cooking.
- For Smoked Meats: add sauce the last 30 to 45 minutes.

GREAT GRILLING RECIPES

In this book, you'll find a wide variety of recipes suited to your grill. We've included everything from tempting appetizers and sizzling main dishes to savory side dishes and heart-warming desserts. The first section, Regional Barbecues, features complete menu suggestions as well as innovative recipes. (Recipes in the menus marked with an asterisk (*) indicate that recipe is included.) The remaining chapters offer you all kinds of recipes to satisfy all your grilling desires. So get the fire started and get ready to enjoy great barbecues—hot off the grill!

REGIONAL BARBECUES

East Coast Fish and Oyster Barbecue

- **Grilled Swordfish***
- **Grilled Tomatoes***
- **Savoy Cabbage Pockets***
- **Mixed Green Salad**
- **Fruit Tart**

To prepare this menu, you'll need to use 60 Kingsford® Charcoal Briquets (about 4 pounds).

GRILLED TOMATOES

Makes 4 servings

2 large tomatoes
2 tablespoons olive oil
1½ teaspoons chopped fresh basil
  or ½ teaspoon dried basil

Salt and pepper

In covered grill, arrange medium-hot **Kingsford® briquets** on one side of grill. Slice each tomato in half crosswise; remove excess juice and seeds. Dip tomato halves in olive oil. Place in foil pan. Place foil pan on edge of grill not directly over briquets. (Swordfish steaks will grill directly over briquets.) Cook tomatoes, on covered grill, 10 to 14 minutes or until heated through. Sprinkle cut surfaces with basil, salt and pepper. Garnish with fresh basil, if desired.

Grilled Tomatoes, Grilled Swordfish (see page 8),
Savoy Cabbage Pockets (see page 8)

GRILLED SWORDFISH

Makes 4 servings

4 fresh or frozen swordfish steaks, ½ inch thick (about 2 pounds)
⅓ cup tomato paste (half of 6-ounce can)
¼ cup dry red wine
6 cloves garlic, sliced
⅛ teaspoon ground red pepper or few dashes hot pepper sauce
3 tablespoons chopped cilantro or parsley
2 tablespoons olive oil

Thaw fish, if frozen. In small bowl, combine tomato paste, wine, garlic and red pepper. Bring to boil on range-top. Reduce heat. Simmer, covered, 1 hour, stirring occasionally. Press through sieve; discard garlic. Stir in cilantro and olive oil. Cool to room temperature.

Place fish in shallow baking dish; brush cooled marinade over fish. Marinate fish 30 minutes at room temperature.

Grill fish, on covered grill, over medium-hot **Kingsford®** briquets 4 minutes; brush with marinade. Turn and cook 3 to 5 minutes longer or until fish flakes easily when tested with fork. Brush again with marinade. Transfer to serving platter.

SAVOY CABBAGE POCKETS

Makes 4 servings

8 to 12 savoy cabbage leaves or green cabbage leaves
¼ cup olive or vegetable oil
1 pint shucked oysters
1 tablespoon chopped fresh thyme or 1 teaspoon dried thyme
Salt and pepper

On range-top, immerse cabbage leaves in boiling water 3 minutes; drain. Remove center vein. Brush cabbage leaves with 2 tablespoons oil. Divide oysters between cabbage leaves; lightly sprinkle with thyme, salt and pepper.

Roll up leaves, jelly-roll style, folding in sides. Brush outer leaves with remaining oil. Place in foil pan, seam-side down. Place uncovered foil pan on grill not directly over coals. Cover grill; cook over medium-hot **Kingsford®** briquets 10 to 15 minutes or until oysters are firm and edges are curled.

Mideast Italian-Style Capon Dinner

- Grilled Capon*
- Creamy Potato Bake*
- Italian-Style Peppers*
- Italian Bread with Butter
- Hot Fruit with Pound Cake*

To prepare this menu, you'll need to use 94 Kingsford® Charcoal Briquets (about 6 pounds).

CREAMY POTATO BAKE

Makes 6 servings

5 medium potatoes, peeled and thinly sliced
1 medium onion, sliced
6 tablespoons butter or margarine
1/3 cup shredded Cheddar cheese
2 tablespoons chopped parsley
1 tablespoon Worcestershire sauce
Salt and pepper
1/3 cup chicken broth

Place sliced potatoes and onion on 22×18-inch piece of heavy-duty foil. Dot with butter. Sprinkle with cheese, parsley, Worcestershire sauce, salt and pepper. Fold up foil around potatoes; add chicken broth. Seal edges tightly.

Grill packet, on covered grill, over medium-hot **Kingsford® briquets** about 35 minutes or until potatoes are tender.

ITALIAN-STYLE PEPPERS

Makes 6 servings

4 large red or green peppers
3 tablespoons olive oil
1 clove garlic, minced
1/8 teaspoon dried oregano, crushed
Salt and pepper

Quarter peppers lengthwise; remove seeds and ribs. Grill peppers, skin-side down, on uncovered grill, over medium-hot **Kingsford® briquets** 6 to 8 minutes or until skins begin to wrinkle and show grill marks. Immediately place under cold running water. Gently pat dry with paper toweling.

Slice peppers into 1/2-inch-wide strips. Heat olive oil in foil pan on grill. Add pepper strips, garlic and oregano. Cover pan with foil. Cook, on covered grill, over medium-hot briquets 15 minutes or until heated through, stirring once. Season to taste with salt and pepper. Serve immediately.

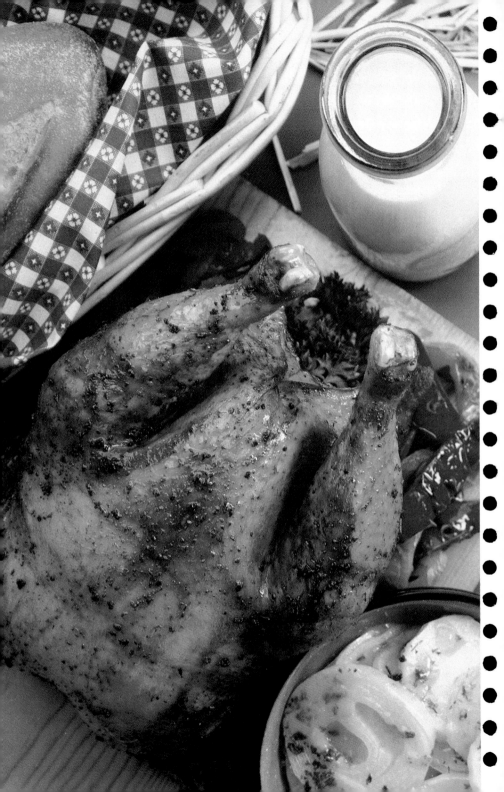

GRILLED CAPON

Makes 6 servings

1 capon or whole roasting
    chicken (6 to 7 pounds)
  Salt
1/4 teaspoon poultry seasoning
1 1/2 medium onions, quartered
1 tablespoon rubbed sage
2 stalks celery with leaves, cut
    into 1-inch pieces

2 medium carrots, cut into
    1/2-inch pieces
2 tablespoons butter or
    margarine, melted
  K.C. Masterpiece® Barbecue
    Sauce

Wash capon thoroughly; pat dry. Rub cavity lightly with salt and poultry seasoning. Insert a few onion quarters in neck and fold neck skin over onion. Fold wings across back with tips touching to secure neck skin. Sprinkle 1 teaspoon sage in body cavity and stuff with remaining onion quarters, the celery and carrots. Tie legs and tail together with string. Insert meat thermometer in center of thigh muscle, not touching bone. Brush skin with melted butter. Rub with remaining sage.

Arrange medium-hot **Kingsford® briquets** around drip pan. Place capon, breast-side up, over drip pan; cover grill and cook 1 1/2 to 2 hours or until thermometer registers 185°F. Tent with heavy-duty foil to prevent overbrowning, if necessary. Brush capon with barbecue sauce during last 10 minutes of cooking. Serve with additional heated barbecue sauce, if desired.

HOT FRUIT WITH POUND CAKE

Makes 6 servings

2 cans (16 ounces each) fruits for
  salad
1/4 cup madeira or port wine
2 tablespoons butter or
  margarine
3/4 teaspoon grated fresh ginger

1 butter pound cake
    (10 3/4 ounces), sliced and
    lightly toasted
  Vanilla ice cream (optional)

Drain fruit; reserve 1/2 cup of syrup. Cut up any large pieces of fruit. In heavy skillet or foil pan, combine fruit, reserved syrup, wine, butter and ginger; place skillet or pan on grill. Heat fruit mixture, on covered grill, over medium-hot **Kingsford® briquets** 15 to 20 minutes or until heated through, stirring once. Spoon warm fruit mixture over toasted pound cake slices. Top each serving with vanilla ice cream, if desired.

Grilled Capon, Italian-Style Peppers (see page 9),
Creamy Potato Bake (see page 9)

Tex-Mex Barbecue Dinner

- Nachos*
- Avocado-Tomato Salad*
- Fajitas*
- Pico de Gallo Sauce*

- Grilled Potatoes*
- Blue Ribbon Pinto Beans*
- Praline Candy or Peanut Brittle

To prepare this menu, you'll need to use 50 Kingsford® Charcoal Briquets (about 3 pounds).

NACHOS

Makes 8 servings

1 bag (8 ounces) tortilla chips
1 can (16 ounces) refried beans
  Pickled jalapeño pepper strips
  (about 24)

2 cups shredded Monterey Jack
  or Cheddar cheese (about
  8 ounces)

Place half the tortilla chips in large iron skillet. Spoon half the beans over chips and arrange jalapeño strips on top. Sprinkle with half the cheese. Make a second layer with remaining ingredients. Grill, on covered grill, over medium-hot **Kingsford® briquets** 6 to 8 minutes or until cheese melts. Serve hot.

AVOCADO-TOMATO SALAD

Makes 8 servings

2 large ripe avocados, seeded
  and peeled
  Lemon juice
2 or 3 medium tomatoes

Lettuce leaves
Prepared Hidden Valley
  Ranch® Original Ranch®
  Salad Dressing Mix

Slice avocados and sprinkle with lemon juice to prevent browning. Cut tomatoes into wedges. Arrange avocado slices and tomato wedges on individual lettuce-lined salad plates. Drizzle with salad dressing.

Avocado-Tomato Salad, Fajitas with
Pico de Gallo Sauce (see page 14), Nachos

FAJITAS

2 pounds boneless beef skirt
  steak or flank steak
¾ cup beer
½ cup lime juice

2 tablespoons Worcestershire
  sauce
8 (6-inch) flour tortillas
  Pico de Gallo Sauce (recipe
  follows)

Trim excess fat from steak; place in shallow glass dish. Combine beer, lime juice and Worcestershire sauce; pour over steak. Cover and refrigerate overnight, spooning marinade over meat occasionally.

Drain steak; reserve marinade. Pat steak dry with paper toweling. Grill steak, on covered grill, over medium-hot **Kingsford® briquets** 8 to 10 minutes, basting meat occasionally with marinade. Turn and grill to desired doneness, allowing 8 to 10 minutes longer for medium. Carve meat across grain into thin slices.

Meanwhile, wrap tortillas in heavy-duty foil; place tortillas at edge of grill 5 minutes or until heated through. Wrap steak slices in warmed tortillas; top with chilled Pico de Gallo Sauce.

PICO DE GALLO SAUCE

Makes about 1¾ cups

3 medium tomatoes, peeled and
  chopped
½ cup chopped green onions
1 large Anaheim chili pepper,
  chopped

1 fresh jalapeño chili pepper,
  seeded and chopped
2 teaspoons chopped fresh
  cilantro or parsley
1 teaspoon salt

In small bowl, combine tomatoes, onions, peppers, cilantro and salt. Cover and refrigerate 5 hours or overnight.

BLUE RIBBON PINTO BEANS

2 pounds dried pinto beans
1 pound sliced smoked bacon,
  cut into 1-inch pieces
2 medium tomatoes, diced
1½ tablespoons ground cumin

1½ tablespoons chili powder
2 medium garlic cloves, minced
1 jalapeño or serrano chili,
  minced
Salt

Place beans in heavy, large saucepan. Cover with water and bring to boil on range-top. Drain. Return beans to pan. Add enough water to cover by 2 to 3 inches. Add remaining ingredients except salt. Bring mixture to boil. Reduce heat to low and simmer until beans are very soft, adding more water, as necessary, to keep beans submerged, about 3½ hours. Season to taste with salt and cook 15 minutes longer, uncovered, if liquid is thin.

GRILLED POTATOES

Makes 8 servings

6 medium potatoes
⅓ cup olive or vegetable oil
¾ teaspoon salt

½ teaspoon garlic powder
¼ teaspoon pepper

Peel potatoes, if desired, and cut each into 4 wedges. In mixing bowl, combine olive oil, salt, garlic powder and pepper. Add cut-up potatoes; toss to coat. Wrap potatoes in heavy-duty foil; seal edges tightly. Grill packet, on edge of covered grill, over medium-hot **Kingsford®** **briquets** about 35 minutes or until potatoes are tender.

Western Rockies Beef Ribs and Fresh Pineapple Barbecue

- Jalapeño Pepper Jelly with Cream Cheese and Assorted Crackers*
- Barbecued Beef Short Ribs*

- Spicy Rice Molds*
- Flaming Pineapple*
- Cabernet Sauvignon

To prepare this menu, you'll need to use about 100 Kingsford® Charcoal Briquets (about 7 pounds).

JALAPEÑO PEPPER JELLY

Makes 6 half-pints

1 large green pepper, cut into quarters
2 fresh jalapeño peppers, seeds and ribs removed
6½ cups sugar

1½ cups cider vinegar
½ of 6-ounce package (1 foil pouch) liquid fruit pectin
Several drops green food coloring (optional)

Finely chop green pepper and jalapeño peppers using a food processor or knife. In 4½-quart Dutch oven, combine green pepper mixture, sugar and vinegar. Bring to boil on range-top; reduce heat. Cover and simmer, stirring often, about 15 minutes or until pepper mixture turns transparent. Stir in pectin; add food coloring, if desired. Return to full rolling boil; boil hard, uncovered, 1 minute, stirring constantly. Remove from heat. Skim off any foam with metal spoon. Pour at once into hot sterilized half-pint jars; seal, using metal lids or paraffin. Serve with cream cheese and assorted crackers.

BARBECUED BEEF SHORT RIBS

Makes 8 servings

6 pounds beef chuck ribs, cut
    into 1-rib pieces
1 cup water
¾ cup soy sauce
⅔ cup dry sherry
½ cup packed dark brown sugar

6 cloves garlic, minced
1 tablespoon cayenne pepper
1 tablespoon grated fresh ginger
2 teaspoons Chinese five spice
    powder

Trim excess fat from ribs. In large roasting pan, arrange ribs in single layer. For marinade, in medium saucepan combine remaining ingredients. Cook over medium heat on range-top until sugar is dissolved. Remove from heat; cool slightly. Pour marinade over ribs. Cover and marinate in refrigerator for 1 hour, turning ribs once.

Cover roasting pan with foil. Arrange medium-hot **Kingsford® briquets** around drip pan. Place roasting pan on grill; cover grill and cook ribs 45 minutes. Remove ribs from roasting pan and continue cooking, in covered grill, 45 to 60 minutes longer or until ribs are tender, turning occasionally. Brush ribs again with marinade just before serving. Reserve ⅓ cup marinade to spoon over Spicy Rice Molds, if desired.

SPICY RICE MOLDS

Makes 8 servings

2⅔ cups water
1⅓ cups long grain rice
  2 tablespoons butter or
    margarine
1½ teaspoons soy sauce
  3 tablespoons chopped green
    onion (optional)

3 tablespoons slivered almonds,
    toasted
2 tablespoons finely chopped
    parsley

In 2-quart saucepan with tight-fitting lid, combine water, rice, butter and soy sauce. Cover. Bring to boil on range-top; reduce heat. Cook 15 minutes; remove from heat. Let stand 10 minutes.

Divide rice mixture between eight buttered ½-cup molds. Unmold onto serving platter. Sprinkle green onion, toasted almonds and parsley on top each. Drizzle with ⅓ cup reserved marinade from Barbecued Beef Short Ribs, if desired.

Flaming Pineapple (see page 18),
Spicy Rice Molds, Barbecued Beef Short Ribs

FLAMING PINEAPPLE

Makes 8 servings

1 fresh pineapple
½ cup packed light brown sugar
½ teaspoon ground cinnamon
⅛ teaspoon freshly ground
   nutmeg

¼ cup butter or margarine
½ cup light rum
   Ice cream, whipped cream or
   chilled soft custard

Cut pineapple in half lengthwise, leaving on green top. Cut each half lengthwise into four sections. Carefully cut pineapple away from peel. Remove core, then cut into 1-inch chunks; rearrange pineapple chunks on peel. Place in large baking pan or foil pan. Sprinkle with brown sugar, cinnamon and nutmeg; dot with butter. Place pan on edge of grill. Heat pineapple, on covered grill, over medium-hot **Kingsford® briquets** 10 minutes; remove pan from grill.

In small saucepan, heat rum on range-top over low heat just until hot. Carefully ignite with match; pour flaming rum over pineapple, stirring sauce and spooning over pineapple. Serve with ice cream, if desired.

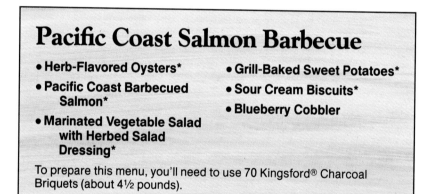

Pacific Coast Salmon Barbecue

- Herb-Flavored Oysters*
- Pacific Coast Barbecued
  Salmon*
- Marinated Vegetable Salad
  with Herbed Salad
  Dressing*
- Grill-Baked Sweet Potatoes*
- Sour Cream Biscuits*
- Blueberry Cobbler

To prepare this menu, you'll need to use 70 Kingsford® Charcoal Briquets (about 4½ pounds).

HERB-FLAVORED OYSTERS

Makes 4 appetizer servings

12 to 16 fresh oysters in shells
½ cup butter or margarine

2 tablespoons lemon juice
2 tablespoons chopped parsley

Thoroughly scrub oysters. Arrange oysters on grid; do not open shells. Grill oysters, on uncovered grill, over medium-hot **Kingsford® briquets** 12 to 15 minutes or until shells steam open. (Discard any oysters that do not open.)

(continued)

Meanwhile, in saucepan, combine butter, lemon juice and parsley. Heat butter mixture on edge of grill until butter is melted, stirring frequently.

Carefully remove cooked oysters from grill and serve hot with lemon-butter mixture spooned over.

PACIFIC COAST BARBECUED SALMON

Makes 4 servings

4 fresh or frozen salmon steaks, 1 inch thick (about 8 ounces each)
½ cup butter or margarine

2 tablespoons fresh lemon juice
1 tablespoon Worcestershire sauce

Thaw salmon steaks, if frozen. In saucepan, combine butter, lemon juice and Worcestershire sauce; simmer 5 minutes, stirring frequently. Brush salmon steaks with butter mixture. Place steaks in well-greased wire grill basket.

Grill steaks, on uncovered grill, over medium-hot **Kingsford® briquets** 6 to 9 minutes or until lightly browned. Baste steaks with butter mixture and turn; grill 6 to 9 minutes longer, basting often, until fish flakes easily when tested with fork.

SOUR CREAM BISCUITS

Makes 8 biscuits

1¼ cups flour
1½ teaspoons baking powder
½ teaspoon salt

¼ teaspoon baking soda
½ cup sour cream
¼ cup light cream or milk

In mixing bowl, stir together flour, baking powder, salt and baking soda. In small bowl, combine sour cream and light cream. Make a well in center of dry ingredients; add sour cream mixture. Stir just until dough clings together and forms a ball.

Knead dough gently on lightly floured surface 10 to 12 strokes. Roll or pat to ½ inch thickness. Cut dough into 2¼-inch rounds.

Using metal spatula, carefully transfer cut biscuits to lightly greased baking sheet. Bake in 375°F oven about 15 minutes or until golden. Serve warm.

MARINATED VEGETABLE SALAD

Makes 4 servings

6 medium carrots, diagonally
  sliced into ¼-inch pieces
1 medium zucchini, cut into
  2-inch julienne strips
1 medium red onion, thinly sliced
  and slices halved

¼ cup chopped red or green
  pepper
1 tablespoon chopped parsley
Herbed Salad Dressing (recipe
  follows)

In large saucepan on range-top, cook carrots, covered, in boiling salted water to cover 2 minutes. Add zucchini; return to boil. Cook, covered, 2 minutes longer or until vegetables are just tender. Drain; rinse with cold water and drain again. Transfer vegetables to bowl. Add onion, red pepper and parsley. Toss with Herbed Salad Dressing. Cover and refrigerate several hours or overnight.

HERBED SALAD DRESSING

Makes ½ cup

¼ cup olive or vegetable oil
¼ cup vinegar
2 tablespoons grated Parmesan
  cheese (optional)

¼ teaspoon dried oregano,
  crushed
¼ teaspoon dried basil, crushed
⅛ teaspoon salt

In screw-top jar, combine all ingredients. Cover and shake well.

GRILL-BAKED SWEET POTATOES

Makes 4 servings

4 medium sweet potatoes
  Oil
4 tablespoons butter or
  margarine

4 tablespoons brown sugar

Tear off four 6×9-inch pieces of heavy-duty foil. Brush sweet potatoes with oil. Pierce several times with fork. Wrap potatoes in foil. Grill potatoes, on uncovered grill, over medium-hot **Kingsford® briquets** about 1 hour or until tender, turning once. Remove foil. Open potatoes with tines of fork and push ends to fluff. Top each with 1 tablespoon butter and 1 tablespoon brown sugar.

Herb-Flavored Oysters (see page 18), Pacific Coast Barbecued Salmon (see page 19), Marinated Vegetable Salad, Sour Cream Biscuits (see page 19)

Rocky Mountain Grilled Cheese and Lamb Riblets Dinner

- Grilled Cheese*
- Western Lamb Riblets*
- Fresh Corn on the Grill*
- Tossed Garden Salad
- Garlic Bread
- Fresh Peach Ice Cream*
- Red Zinfandel

To prepare this menu, you'll need to use 60 Kingsford® Charcoal Briquets (about 4 pounds).

GRILLED CHEESE

Makes 6 servings

1 piece raclette cheese (12 to 16 ounces)
1 tablespoon olive oil

½ teaspoon ground oregano
Sliced crusty French bread or large crackers

Place cheese in 10-inch iron skillet; brush with olive oil. Sprinkle oregano on top. Place some bread slices around cheese in skillet.

Grill cheese, on covered grill, over medium-hot **Kingsford® briquets** 10 minutes or until cheese is very soft. Remove to table; spread cheese on bread slices.

Note: Raclette cheese is available at specialty cheese shops. You can try another soft cheese, such as Swiss, but cooking time may vary.

FRESH CORN ON THE GRILL

Makes 6 servings

6 ears corn, with silk and husks intact

Butter or margarine
Salt and pepper

Turn back corn husks; do not remove. Remove silks with stiff brush; rinse corn. Lay husks back into position. Roast ears, on covered grill, over medium-hot **Kingsford® briquets** about 25 minutes or until tender, turning corn often. Remove husks and serve with butter, salt and pepper, as desired.

Grilled Cheese, Fresh Corn on the Grill, Western Lamb Riblets (see page 24)

WESTERN LAMB RIBLETS

Makes 6 servings

5 pounds lamb riblets, cut into
  serving-size pieces
¾ cup chili sauce
½ cup honey
½ cup beer

¼ cup Worcestershire sauce
¼ cup finely chopped onion
1 clove garlic, minced
½ teaspoon crushed red pepper

Trim excess fat from riblets. In saucepan, combine chili sauce, honey, beer, Worcestershire, onion, garlic and red pepper. On range-top, heat mixture to boiling. Reduce heat; simmer, covered, 10 minutes. Remove from heat; cool.

Place riblets in plastic bag; pour marinade over riblets. Close bag; set bag in large bowl. Marinate riblets in refrigerator about 2 hours, turning bag occasionally to distribute marinade evenly.

Drain riblets; reserve marinade. Arrange medium-hot **Kingsford®** briquets around drip pan. Place riblets over drip pan. Cover grill and cook 45 minutes, turning riblets and brushing with marinade twice. Heat remaining marinade and serve with riblets.

FRESH PEACH ICE CREAM

Makes 3 quarts

¾ cup sugar
1 envelope unflavored gelatin
  Dash salt
4 cups light cream
1 egg, beaten
2 teaspoons vanilla

3 pounds fully ripe peaches,
  peeled and mashed
  (4½ cups)
½ cup sugar
¼ teaspoon ground mace or
  ¼ teaspoon almond extract

In large saucepan, combine the ¾ cup sugar, gelatin and salt. Stir in half of the cream. On range-top, cook and stir over medium heat until gelatin mixture almost boils and sugar dissolves.

Stir about ½ cup hot gelatin mixture into beaten egg; return mixture to saucepan. Cook and stir 2 minutes longer. Cool. Stir in remaining cream and vanilla.

Stir together mashed peaches, the ½ cup sugar and mace. Add to cooled egg mixture; mix well.

Freeze in 4- or 5-quart ice cream freezer according to manufacturer's directions.

Western Chestnuts and Tenderloin Barbecue

- Roasted Chestnuts*
- Grilled Tenderloin with Cognac and Garlic Mushrooms*

- Scalloped Potatoes
- Fresh Blackberry Cobbler*
- Burgundy

To prepare this menu, you'll need to use 70 Kingsford® Charcoal Briquets (about 4½ pounds).

GRILLED TENDERLOIN WITH COGNAC

Makes 8 servings

1 beef tenderloin (2 pounds)
¼ cup whole green, white or black peppercorns
Garlic Mushrooms (recipe follows)
⅓ cup cognac or other brandy
1 cup whipping cream

2 tablespoons Dijon-style mustard
1 tablespoon Worcestershire sauce
2 teaspoons lemon juice

Trim excess fat from roast. Coarsely crack peppercorns with mortar and pestle; sprinkle on roast and press into surface.

Arrange medium-hot **Kingsford® briquets** around drip pan. Place roast over drip pan. Cover grill and cook, turning once, until meat thermometer registers 140°F for rare (about 45 minutes), 150°F for medium-rare (about 50 minutes), 160°F for medium (about 55 minutes) or 170°F for well-done (about 60 minutes). While roast is cooking, prepare Garlic Mushrooms. About 15 minutes before meat is done, place mushrooms next to meat.

When roast is grilled to desired doneness, warm cognac in skillet on range-top. Remove from heat. Place roast in heated skillet. Carefully ignite with a match; allow flames to subside, carefully spooning cognac over meat. Remove roast to grated serving platter; reserve juices.

In saucepan on range-top, combine cream, mustard and Worcestershire sauce. Bring to boil. Cook and stir 3 minutes over medium-low heat until slightly thickened. Remove from heat; stir in lemon juice and reserved cognac juices. Carve roast and arrange with Garlic Mushrooms. Pour cream sauce over sliced roast and mushrooms. Garnish with fresh rosemary, if desired.

GARLIC MUSHROOMS

Makes 8 servings

32 large fresh mushrooms
½ cup olive or vegetable oil

2 cloves garlic, minced

Remove stems from mushrooms; reserve caps. In bowl, combine olive oil and garlic; add mushroom caps. Gently toss to coat. Remove mushrooms with slotted spoon; place mushroom caps on piece of heavy-duty foil. Seal edges tightly. Grill at side of roast 10 to 15 minutes or until tender.

ROASTED CHESTNUTS

Makes 8 servings

4 cups chestnuts

Using a sharp knife, make an × on flat side of each chestnut. Place nuts in 13×9×2-inch baking pan or in foil pan. Grill chestnuts, on covered grill, over medium-hot **Kingsford® briquets** 10 to 15 minutes or until skin begins to lift away from nuts, stirring once. Peel outer skin while still warm.

FRESH BLACKBERRY COBBLER

Makes 8 servings

4 cups whole blackberries or blueberries
½ cup sugar
2 tablespoons butter or margarine

1 cup packaged biscuit mix
2 tablespoons sugar
⅓ cup light cream
Vanilla ice cream

In 10-inch heavy skillet with tight-fitting lid, combine blackberries and ½ cup sugar. Dot with butter. Cook and stir on range-top, over medium heat, until bubbly. Keep hot.

Prepare biscuit topper. In medium mixing bowl, combine biscuit mix, 2 tablespoons sugar and light cream; mix well. Spoon biscuit batter in 8 mounds over hot berry mixture.

Cover skillet and place on edge of grill over medium-hot **Kingsford® briquets**. Cook, on covered grill, over medium-hot briquets about 15 minutes or until done. Serve warm with vanilla ice cream.

Roasted Chestnuts, Grilled Tenderloin with Cognac (see page 25), Garlic Mushrooms, Fresh Blackberry Cobbler

Midwest Pork Chops and Fruit Barbecue

- **Barbecued Pork Chops***
- **Corn-Pepper-Sausage Skillet***
- **Apple Slaw***
- **Strawberries 'n Cream***

To prepare this menu, you'll need to use 50 Kingsford® Charcoal Briquets (about 3 pounds).

BARBECUED PORK CHOPS

Makes 6 servings

6 pork loin chops, cut 1 inch thick
½ teaspoon seasoned salt
6 slices orange

6 thin slices onion
6 thin slices lemon
⅓ cup K.C. Masterpiece®
   Barbecue Sauce

Arrange medium-hot **Kingsford® briquets** to one side of grill with drip pan next to briquets. Sprinkle chops with seasoned salt. Place chops over drip pan; cover grill and cook 40 minutes or until nearly done, turning once after 25 minutes.

Top each chop with slices of orange, onion, lemon and about 1 tablespoon barbecue sauce. Cover grill and cook 5 to 10 minutes longer or until chops are tender and thoroughly cooked.

APPLE SLAW

Makes 6 servings

2 red apples, chopped
1 tablespoon lemon juice
1 small head cabbage, shredded
   (about 5 cups)

¾ cup prepared Hidden Valley
   Ranch® Original Ranch®
   Salad Dressing Mix
Pepper

In bowl, toss chopped apples with lemon juice. Add cabbage and dressing; toss to thoroughly coat. Season to taste with pepper. Cover; chill before serving.

Corn-Pepper-Sausage Skillet (see page 30),
Apple Slaw, Barbecued Pork Chops

CORN-PEPPER-SAUSAGE SKILLET

Makes 6 servings

12 ounces Italian sausage or bulk
  pork sausage
1 cup chopped green or red
  pepper
1 cup chopped onion
3 cups fresh whole kernel corn or
  1 package (16 ounces)
  frozen whole kernel corn,
  thawed

½ teaspoon garlic salt
¼ teaspoon black pepper
¼ teaspoon chili powder
¼ teaspoon ground cumin
Halved cherry tomatoes
  (optional)
Herbed cream cheese,
  softened (optional)
Sprig parsley (optional)

Crumble sausage into heavy 10-inch skillet or heavy aluminum foil pan. Add green pepper and onion. Place skillet, on covered grill, over medium-hot **Kingsford® briquets** about 15 minutes or until meat is browned, stirring once or twice. Remove from grill; carefully drain off fat.

Stir in corn, garlic salt, pepper, chili powder and cumin; mix well. Cover skillet with foil. Continue grilling, on covered grill, over medium-hot briquets, 10 minutes longer or until heated through. Garnish with tomato halves spread with cream cheese; top with parsley sprig.

STRAWBERRIES 'N CREAM

Makes 6 servings

2 pints (4 cups) fresh
  strawberries, hulled and
  halved

¼ cup honey
2 tablespoons orange liqueur
1 quart vanilla ice cream

Arrange strawberries on 20×18-inch piece of heavy-duty foil. In small bowl, combine honey and liqueur. Drizzle over strawberries. Fold foil loosely around berries; seal edges tightly.

Grill packet, on covered grill, over medium-hot **Kingsford® briquets** 10 to 12 minutes or until fruit is heated through. (If briquets have cooled to medium, grill fruit 12 to 15 minutes or until hot.) Serve hot over vanilla ice cream.

Southern Spicy Ribs and Fruit Dinner

- Pork Spareribs*
- Hot Apple Salad*
- Grilled Potato Hash*
- Corn Muffins (see page 43)
- Fruit Kabobs with Whiskey Baste*

To prepare this menu, you'll need to use 80 Kingsford® Charcoal Briquets (about 5 pounds).

HOT APPLE SALAD

Makes 4 servings

2 red cooking apples, cored and thinly sliced (2 cups)
3 cups finely shredded red cabbage
4 teaspoons butter or margarine, cut up

3 tablespoons rice wine vinegar
4 teaspoons sugar
¾ teaspoon salt
¼ teaspoon caraway seed

In mixing bowl, toss together all ingredients. Turn out onto 18×24-inch piece of heavy-duty foil. Fold edges around apple mixture; seal edges tightly. Grill packet, on covered grill, over medium-hot **Kingsford® briquets** 45 minutes or until apples are tender, turning packet every 15 minutes.

PORK SPARERIBS

Makes 4 servings

4 pounds pork spareribs or pork loin back ribs

1¼ cups K.C. Masterpiece® Barbecue Sauce

Remove breast section from ribs, if desired. Cut ribs into 4 to 5 rib portions. Arrange medium-hot **Kingsford® briquets** around drip pan. Place ribs over drip pan; cover grill and cook 1¼ hours. Turn; brush with barbecue sauce. Continue grilling, on covered grill, 10 to 15 minutes longer or until ribs are thoroughly cooked, brushing once or twice. Heat remaining sauce to serve with ribs, if desired.

GRILLED POTATO HASH

Makes 4 servings

2 tablespoons butter or
   margarine
2 tablespoons all-purpose flour
¾ teaspoon salt
¼ teaspoon seasoned pepper
⅛ teaspoon celery seed

1 cup milk
4 medium potatoes, peeled and
   cut into cubes
1 cup chopped onion
½ cup chopped green pepper
¼ teaspoon paprika

In medium saucepan, melt butter on range-top. Blend in flour, salt, seasoned pepper and celery seed. Stir in milk all at once. Cook and stir over medium heat until thickened and bubbly. Cook and stir 1 minute longer.

Add potatoes, onion and green pepper. Turn potato mixture out onto 18×24-inch piece of heavy-duty foil; sprinkle with paprika. Fold foil loosely around potato mixture and seal edges tightly.

Grill packet, on covered grill, over medium-hot **Kingsford® briquets** 45 to 50 minutes or until potatoes are tender, turning packet every 15 minutes.

FRUIT KABOBS WITH WHISKEY BASTE

Makes 4 servings

2 tablespoons honey
2 tablespoons whiskey
1 tablespoon lemon juice
1 can (8 ounces) pineapple
   chunks, drained

1 large banana, diagonally sliced
   into 1-inch pieces
1 orange, peeled and sectioned
8 maraschino cherries

In mixing bowl, combine honey, whiskey and lemon juice; add pineapple chunks, banana pieces, orange sections and cherries. Gently toss to coat fruit well. Cover and refrigerate up to 2 hours or until ready to grill.

Remove fruit with slotted spoon, reserving the whiskey baste to brush on fruit kabobs while grilling. Alternately thread fruit onto skewers.

Grill fruit kabobs, on covered grill, over medium-low **Kingsford® briquets** 5 to 10 minutes or until fruit is warmed through.

Pork Spareribs (see page 31), Fruit Kabobs
with Whiskey Baste, Hot Apple Salad (see page 31)

Southwest Mexican Chicken Barbecue

- Over-the-Coals Spiced Popcorn*
- Mexican Chicken with Spicy Bacon*
- Punched Potatoes*
- Charcoal-Grilled Tortillas
- Charcoal-Baked Bananas Flambé*
- Mexican Beer or Iced Tea

To prepare this menu, you'll need to use 84 Kingsford® Charcoal Briquets (about 5½ pounds).

OVER-THE-COALS SPICED POPCORN

Makes about 8 cups

½ cup popcorn or 8 cups popped popcorn
2 tablespoons butter or margarine
½ teaspoon Worcestershire sauce
½ teaspoon chili powder
½ teaspoon lemon pepper
¼ teaspoon garlic powder
¼ teaspoon onion powder
⅛ teaspoon salt

If desired, pop ½ cup popcorn over briquets in long-handled fireplace corn popper. Hold directly over, but not touching, hot **Kingsford® briquets**; shake vigorously until corn is popped, about 3 to 4 minutes.

In saucepan, combine remaining ingredients. Set on edge of grill to melt butter. Toss butter mixture with popped popcorn.

PUNCHED POTATOES

Makes 4 servings

4 medium baking potatoes
Lard or shortening
Butter or margarine
Salt and pepper

Scrub potatoes; pierce several times with fork. For soft skins, rub with lard. Grill potatoes, on covered grill, over medium-hot **Kingsford® briquets** about 55 minutes or until tender, turning occasionally. Open with tines of fork; push ends together to fluff. Top with butter and season to taste.

Charcoal-Baked Bananas Flambé,
Mexican Chicken with Spicy Bacon (see page 36)

MEXICAN CHICKEN WITH SPICY BACON

Makes 4 servings

2 serrano chili peppers
2 cloves garlic
  Dash ground cloves
  Dash ground cinnamon

4 slices bacon, partially cooked
1 whole roasting chicken (3½ to
  4 pounds)

Remove stems from peppers. Slit open; remove seeds and ribs. Finely chop peppers and garlic. Place in small bowl. Stir in cloves and cinnamon. Cut bacon into 1-inch pieces.

Lift skin layer of chicken at neck cavity. Insert hand, lifting skin from meat along breast, thigh and drumstick. Using small metal spatula, spread pepper mixture evenly over meat, under skin. Place a layer of bacon pieces over pepper mixture. Skewer neck skin to back. Tie legs securely to tail and twist wing tips under back of chicken. Insert meat thermometer in center of thigh muscle, not touching bone.

Arrange medium-hot **Kingsford®** **briquets** around drip pan. Place chicken, breast-side up, over drip pan. Cover grill and cook about 1 hour or until meat thermometer registers 185°F. Garnish with cherry tomatoes and serrano chili peppers, if desired.

CHARCOAL-BAKED BANANAS FLAMBÉ

Makes 4 servings

4 ripe medium bananas
4 tablespoons butter or
  margarine
½ cup packed brown sugar
¼ teaspoon ground allspice or
  ½ teaspoon ground
  cinnamon or freshly grated
  nutmeg

¼ cup lime juice
¼ cup dark rum

Grill unpeeled bananas, on covered grill, over medium-hot **Kingsford®** **briquets** about 8 minutes or until just barely tender and darkened in color. Remove from grill.

In 10-inch oven-proof skillet, combine butter, brown sugar and desired spice. Heat directly over medium-hot briquets 2 to 3 minutes or until mixture is bubbly. Stir in lime juice.

(continued)

Slit bananas lengthwise; do not remove peel. Arrange bananas in the 10-inch skillet. Continue to grill, on uncovered grill, 6 to 8 minutes or until sauce thickens slightly and bananas are tender, spooning sauce over bananas occasionally. Remove skillet from grill.

In small saucepan, heat rum on range-top over low heat just until hot. Carefully ignite with a match and pour flaming rum over bananas in skillet. When flame subsides, serve bananas with sauce spooned over.

Northwest Grilled Cornish Game Hens and Vegetable Dinner

- Grilled Cornish Game Hens*
- Rice Pilaf with Sauteed Pecans*
- Skewered Vegetables*
- Fresh Fruit Salad
- Baked Honey Apples*

To prepare this menu, you'll need to use 65 Kingsford® Charcoal Briquets (about 4 pounds).

GRILLED CORNISH GAME HENS

Makes 4 servings

2 Cornish game hens (1 to 1½ pounds each)
3 tablespoons olive oil
⅓ cup lemon juice

1 tablespoon black peppercorns, coarsely crushed
½ teaspoon salt
Sprig fresh rosemary

Split hens lengthwise. Rinse hen halves; pat dry with paper toweling.

For marinade, in small bowl combine olive oil, lemon juice, peppercorns and salt. Place hen halves in large plastic bag. Set in bowl. Pour marinade over hens. Close bag and refrigerate several hours or overnight, turning hen halves occasionally to coat with marinade.

Arrange medium-hot **Kingsford® briquets** around drip pan. Just before grilling, add rosemary sprig to coals. Remove hens from marinade and place, skin-side up, over drip pan. Cover grill and cook 45 minutes or until thigh moves easily and juices run clear. Baste with marinade occasionally. Garnish with fresh rosemary, if desired.

RICE PILAF WITH SAUTEED PECANS

Makes 4 servings

⅓ cup wild rice
2⅔ cups water
  1 teaspoon instant chicken
     bouillon granules
  1 cup long grain rice

½ cup coarsely chopped pecans
3 tablespoons butter or
  margarine
2 tablespoons chopped parsley

Run cold water over wild rice in strainer about 1 minute, lifting wild rice to rinse well.

In 2-quart saucepan with tight-fitting lid, combine water, wild rice and chicken bouillon granules. Bring to boil on range-top. Reduce heat. Cover and simmer 20 minutes. Add long grain rice; return to boil. Reduce heat and simmer, covered, 20 to 25 minutes or until rice is tender and water is absorbed.

Meanwhile, in small skillet, sauté pecans in butter about 2 minutes or until golden. Add pecans to hot rice mixture; stir in parsley. Toss lightly until combined. Serve immediately.

SKEWERED VEGETABLES

Makes 4 servings

2 medium zucchini, cut into
  1½-inch slices
8 small boiling onions
8 fresh medium mushrooms

2 tablespoons butter or
  margarine, melted
4 cherry tomatoes
Salt and pepper

Cook zucchini and onions in boiling water on range-top, covered, 1 minute. Remove onions with slotted spoon. Cook zucchini 4 minutes longer; remove and drain. On four skewers, alternately thread zucchini, onions and mushrooms. Brush with butter.

Grill vegetables, on covered grill, over medium-hot **Kingsford®** briquets 6 minutes or until tender, carefully turning skewers once. Add cherry tomatoes to tip of skewers during last minute of grilling. Season to taste with salt and pepper. Serve immediately.

Grilled Cornish Game Hens (see page 37), Skewered Vegetables,
Rice Pilaf with Sauteed Pecans, Baked Honey Apples (see page 40)

BAKED HONEY APPLES

Makes 4 servings

**2 to 3 apples, cored and sliced
into ¾-inch rings**

**½ cup butter or margarine
⅓ cup honey**

Arrange 2 or 3 apple rings on four 12×12-inch pieces of heavy-duty foil. Dot with butter; drizzle with honey. Fold foil loosely around apples; seal edges. Grill packets, on covered grill, over medium-hot **Kingsford® briquets** 12 to 15 minutes or until apples are crisp-tender, turning packets once.

Gulf Coast Shrimp and Mushroom Barbecue

- **Sauteed Mushrooms in Garlic Butter***
- **Bacon-Wrapped Shrimp***
- **Mexican Fried Rice***
- **Grilled Zucchini***
- **Coconut Meringue Pie**

To prepare this menu, you'll need to use 45 Kingsford® Charcoal Briquets (about 3 pounds).

SAUTEED MUSHROOMS IN GARLIC BUTTER

Makes 6 servings

**¼ cup butter or margarine
¼ cup white wine vinegar
½ teaspoon garlic powder
¼ teaspoon salt
⅛ teaspoon freshly cracked
pepper**

**6 cups fresh mushrooms
(1 pound)
1 small red onion, thinly sliced
and separated into rings
Chopped parsley**

In heavy 10-inch skillet, melt butter, on uncovered grill, directly over medium-hot **Kingsford® briquets**. Stir in vinegar, garlic powder, salt and pepper; add whole mushrooms and onion rings. Cover skillet; cook vegetables 10 minutes. Stir vegetables and cook 10 minutes longer. Sprinkle with parsley before serving.

*Sauteed Mushrooms in Garlic Butter, Bacon-Wrapped
Shrimp (see page 42), Mexican Fried Rice (see page 43)*

BACON-WRAPPED SHRIMP

Makes 6 servings

1 pound fresh or frozen shrimp,
 shelled and deveined
1 small onion, finely chopped
½ cup olive or vegetable oil
½ teaspoon sugar
½ teaspoon red pepper
¼ teaspoon salt

¼ teaspoon dried oregano,
 crushed
½ teaspoon garlic powder
½ pound bacon
 Mexican Fried Rice (recipe
 follows)

Thaw shrimp, if frozen. For marinade, in small mixing bowl combine the next seven ingredients. Place shrimp in plastic bag; set in deep bowl. Pour marinade over shrimp; close bag. Marinate shrimp 3 hours in refrigerator or 1 hour at room temperature, turning occasionally.

Halve bacon slices lengthwise and crosswise. In large skillet on range-top, partially cook bacon. Drain on paper toweling. Drain shrimp; reserve marinade. Wrap bacon strips around shrimp and secure with wooden picks. Place shrimp in wire grill basket or on 12×9-inch piece of heavy-duty foil. (If using foil, puncture foil in several places.)

Grill shrimp, on uncovered grill, over medium-hot **Kingsford®** briquets 12 minutes or until bacon and shrimp are done, turning basket or individual shrimp once and basting with marinade. Serve with Mexican Fried Rice.

GRILLED ZUCCHINI

Makes 6 servings

3 medium zucchini
 Desired seasonings: basil,
 oregano, thyme, dill weed,
 lemon pepper, grated
 Parmesan cheese, celery
 salt or garlic salt

2 to 3 tablespoons butter or
 margarine, softened

Cut zucchini in half lengthwise. Sprinkle three halves with desired seasoning. Spread butter on remaining three halves. Place seasoned and buttered halves together; cut crosswise and wrap individual servings in heavy-duty foil. Grill zucchini, on uncovered grill, over medium-hot **Kingsford®** briquets 15 to 20 minutes or until tender, turning often.

MEXICAN FRIED RICE

Makes 6 servings

3 tablespoons vegetable oil
1 cup long grain rice
2 cups water
1 cup chili salsa

½ cup chopped green pepper
1 small onion, chopped
1 clove garlic, minced

In 12-inch skillet, heat oil. Add rice; cook until golden brown, stirring often. Stir in remaining ingredients. Bring mixture to boil; reduce heat. Cover; simmer 15 to 20 minutes or until rice is tender. Season to taste; serve additional salsa, if desired.

Southeast Pork Barbecue

- **Barbecued Pork Leg***
- **Sam's Mop Sauce***
- **Southern-Style Squash and Okra***
- **Saucy New Potatoes***
- **Corn Muffins***
- **Peaches in Port***

To prepare this menu, you'll need to use about 134 Kingsford® Charcoal Briquets (about 8 pounds).

CORN MUFFINS

Makes about 14 muffins

1 cup all-purpose flour
1 cup yellow cornmeal
¼ cup sugar
4 teaspoons baking powder
¾ teaspoon salt

2 eggs
1 cup milk
¼ cup vegetable oil or shortening, melted

In mixing bowl, stir together flour, cornmeal, sugar, baking powder and salt. Add eggs, milk and oil. Beat just until combined; do not overbeat.

Grease muffin cups or line with paper baking cups; fill ⅔ full. Bake in 400°F oven 15 to 20 minutes or until done. Let stand 3 minutes in pan. Loosen muffins; remove from pan.

BARBECUED PORK LEG

Makes about 20 servings

1 fresh pork leg, skinned, boned, trimmed of fat, rolled and tied (14 to 16 pounds)

Sam's Mop Sauce (recipe follows)
K.C. Masterpiece® Hickory Barbecue Sauce

Arrange medium-hot **Kingsford® briquets** around drip pan. Place prepared pork leg over drip pan; cover grill and cook pork 4 to 4½ hours or until thermometer inserted in thickest portion registers 170°F. Baste pork with Sam's Mop Sauce every 30 minutes, patting a thin coating of sauce on meat with a cotton swab mop or pastry brush. Let stand, covered with foil, 10 minutes before serving.

Meanwhile, in saucepan, combine half the remaining Mop Sauce with an equal amount of barbecue sauce. Heat through and serve with slices of pork.

Note: The final weight of the fresh pork leg for grilling should be 8 to 10 pounds. To save time, you can have the butcher prepare the fresh pork leg for you.

SAM'S MOP SAUCE

Makes 2¼ cups

1 lemon
1 cup water
1 cup cider vinegar
1 tablespoon butter or margarine
1 tablespoon olive oil
½ teaspoon ground red pepper

1½ to 3 teaspoons hot pepper sauce
1½ to 3 teaspoons Worcestershire sauce
1½ teaspoons black pepper

With vegetable peeler, remove peel from lemon; squeeze juice from lemon. In heavy saucepan, combine lemon peel, juice and remaining ingredients. Bring to boil. Place saucepan on grill to keep warm, if space permits.

Corn Muffins (see page 43), Peaches in Port (see page 46), Barbecued Pork Leg with Sam's Mop Sauce

SOUTHERN-STYLE SQUASH AND OKRA

Makes 4 to 6 servings

2 small onions, sliced and
    separated into rings
3 medium crookneck squash, cut
    into ¼-inch slices
1 package (10 ounces) frozen
    whole okra, thawed and cut
    into bite-size pieces
2 tablespoons butter or margarine

1 clove garlic, minced
1 teaspoon salt
⅛ teaspoon pepper
½ teaspoon dried thyme, crushed
1 tablespoon lemon juice
¼ cup grated Cheddar cheese
    (1 ounce)

Place sliced onions, squash and okra on 24×18-inch piece of heavy-duty foil. Dot with butter. Sprinkle with garlic, salt, pepper, thyme and lemon juice. Fold and seal foil edges tightly. Grill packet, on covered grill, over medium-hot **Kingsford® briquets** 25 to 30 minutes or until tender, turning packet over once. To serve, unwrap foil packet and sprinkle with Cheddar cheese.

SAUCY NEW POTATOES

Makes 4 to 6 servings

1½ pounds new potatoes
½ cup K.C. Masterpiece® Hickory
    Barbecue Sauce

¼ cup water
  Salt and pepper

Cut largest potatoes in half; arrange on 18×18-inch piece of heavy-duty foil. Mix barbecue sauce with water; pour over potatoes. Season to taste with salt and pepper. Fold foil over potatoes and crimp edges together to seal. Grill packet, on covered grill, over medium-hot **Kingsford® briquets** about 30 minutes or until potatoes are tender. Turn packet over after 15 minutes.

PEACHES IN PORT

Makes 4 to 6 servings

6 to 8 large fresh peaches,
    peeled and cut into sixths
2 teaspoons lemon juice

¼ cup tawny port wine
2 tablespoons butter or
    margarine

Arrange peaches on 24×18-inch piece of heavy-duty foil. Sprinkle with lemon juice and port; dot with butter. Fold foil loosely around fruit and seal edges tightly. Grill packet, on covered grill, over medium-hot **Kingsford®** **briquets** about 15 minutes or until fruit is hot, turning packet over once.

Northeast Barbecued Lamb Dinner

- Skewered Shrimp with Lemon*
- Butterflied Leg of Lamb*
- Grill-Roasted Onions*
- Vegetable-Rice Salad*
- Cranberry Cake

To prepare this menu, you'll need to use 72 Kingsford® Charcoal Briquets (about 5 pounds).

SKEWERED SHRIMP WITH LEMON

Makes 8 appetizer servings

16 fresh or frozen large shrimp, shelled and deveined
½ cup olive or vegetable oil
2 lemons
½ cup fine dry bread crumbs
½ teaspoon pepper

Thaw shrimp, if frozen. Thread 2 shrimp on each of 8 skewers. Brush with 2 tablespoons oil. Finely shred lemon peels. In bowl, combine lemon peel, bread crumbs and ¼ teaspoon pepper. Press crumb mixture firmly onto shrimp to coat evenly.

Meanwhile, for dipping sauce, squeeze juice from lemons (you should have about 6 tablespoons juice). Combine juice with remaining oil and pepper. Set mixture aside.

A half-hour before serving, grill breaded shrimp, on covered grill, over medium-hot **Kingsford® briquets** 4 minutes. Turn skewers, continue grilling 4 minutes longer or until shrimp are pink and crumbs are slightly browned. Serve shrimp with lemony dipping sauce.

VEGETABLE-RICE SALAD

Makes 8 servings

3 cups cooked long grain rice
1¾ cups prepared Hidden Valley Ranch® Original Ranch® Salad Dressing Mix
2 medium tomatoes, chopped
Milk
Lettuce
Cooked green beans (optional)

In bowl, combine rice and salad dressing. Toss gently to coat. Cover; chill. Just before serving, stir in tomatoes. Stir in 2 to 3 tablespoons milk if rice mixture seems dry. Turn into a lettuce-lined salad bowl. Garnish with beans and additional chopped tomato, if desired.

BUTTERFLIED LEG OF LAMB

Makes 8 to 10 servings

1 leg of lamb (6 pounds), boned
  and butterflied
2 cloves garlic, minced
1 tablespoon cracked
  peppercorns
½ cup olive or vegetable oil
4 teaspoons Dijon-style mustard

½ cup chopped fresh mint or
  2 tablespoons dried mint
1 tablespoon chopped fresh
  rosemary or 1 teaspoon dried
  rosemary, crushed
1½ teaspoons finely shredded
  lemon peel

Remove excess fat and thin fat covering from surface of lamb. Pound meat to even thickness, about 1½ inches. Place lamb in large plastic bag. Place bag in shallow roasting pan. Combine remaining ingredients; pour over lamb. Close bag. Marinate lamb 2 to 5 days in refrigerator, turning occasionally.

Arrange medium-hot **Kingsford® briquets** around drip pan. Drain meat; reserve marinade. Put 2 skewers diagonally through meat to keep flat while grilling. Insert meat thermometer in thickest part of meat. Place lamb over drip pan. Cover grill and cook 35 to 40 minutes or until thermometer registers 140°F for rare (grill 45 minutes for medium doneness, 160°F). Brush with marinade often. Remove meat; let stand, covered, 15 minutes. Slice meat thinly to serve.

GRILL-ROASTED ONIONS

Makes 8 servings

4 medium yellow onions,
  unpeeled
1 tablespoon olive or vegetable
  oil

Salt and pepper
8 teaspoons butter or margarine

Cut unpeeled onions in half through stem ends. Brush onions with olive oil. Place onion halves on 18×18-inch piece of heavy-duty foil. Season to taste with salt and pepper. Place 1 teaspoon butter on each onion half. Wrap loosely in foil; seal edges tightly.

Grill packet, on covered grill, over medium-hot **Kingsford® briquets** 20 minutes or until onions are tender, turning foil packet once. Unwrap packet and serve onions in skins.

Butterflied Leg of Lamb, Grill-Roasted Onions,
Vegetable-Rice Salad (see page 47)

KINGSFORD®

BEEF

SIRLOIN STEAK WITH KABOBS

Makes 4 servings

1 beef sirloin steak, cut 1 inch
   thick (about 2 pounds)
Salt and pepper

Vegetable Kabobs (recipe
   follows)

Grill steak, on covered grill, over medium-hot **Kingsford**® **briquets** 7 to 8
minutes. Turn steak; season with salt and pepper. Cover grill and continue
cooking 8 to 9 minutes longer or until steak is done as desired. Serve with
Vegetable Kabobs.

VEGETABLE KABOBS

Makes 4 servings

½ cup butter or margarine
1 tablespoon chopped parsley
1 teaspoon chopped fresh basil
½ teaspoon dried oregano
½ teaspoon salt

¼ teaspoon pepper
1 medium zucchini, cut into
   8 slices
8 large mushrooms
8 large cherry tomatoes

Melt butter in small saucepan; add parsley, basil, oregano, salt and pepper.
Cook over low heat 2 to 3 minutes. Thread 2 slices zucchini and 2
mushrooms onto each of four 12-inch skewers. Brush both sides of
vegetables with seasoned butter. Grill kabobs, on uncovered grill, over
medium-hot **Kingsford**® **briquets** 15 minutes, turning and brushing kabobs
occasionally with seasoned butter. Place 2 cherry tomatoes on ends of each
skewer during last 5 minutes of grilling.

*Favorite recipe from **Beef Industry Council***

Sirloin Steak with Vegetable Kabobs

Honey-Mustard Beef Ribs

HONEY-MUSTARD BEEF RIBS

Makes 4 servings

1 cup butter or margarine
1 bunch green onions with tops, finely chopped
1 small yellow onion, finely chopped
4 cloves garlic, minced

4 tablespoons prepared mustard
4 tablespoons honey
½ teaspoon liquid smoke
1 teaspoon lemon pepper
1 teaspoon brown sugar
5 pounds beef back ribs

Combine butter, green onions, yellow onion and garlic in saucepan. Cook over low heat 15 minutes or until onions are transparent. Remove from heat and add remaining ingredients, except ribs. Grill ribs, on covered grill, over medium-hot **Kingsford® briquets** 30 to 35 minutes, brushing ribs generously with mustard-honey mixture, until meat is tender.

ISLANDER'S BEEF BARBECUE

Makes 4 to 6 servings

3 to 3½ pounds boneless beef
    chuck roast
¾ cup apricot-pineapple jam

2 tablespoons soy sauce
1 teaspoon ground ginger
1 teaspoon grated lemon peel

Slice roast across grain into ¼-inch thick slices. Combine remaining ingredients in bowl; mix well. Grill beef slices, on uncovered grill, over medium-hot **Kingsford® briquets** 8 to 10 minutes. Turn and baste often with jam mixture.

Note: If time permits, pierce meat several times with fork and marinate in jam mixture 1 to 4 hours before grilling.

NUTTY BURGERS

Makes 6 servings

1½ pounds ground beef
1 medium onion, finely chopped
1 clove garlic, finely chopped
1 cup dry bread crumbs
⅓ cup grated Parmesan cheese

⅔ cup pine nuts
⅓ cup chopped fresh parsley
2 eggs
1½ teaspoons salt
1 teaspoon pepper

Combine all ingredients; blend well. Shape into 6 thick patties. Grill patties, on covered grill, over medium-hot **Kingsford® briquets** 5 minutes on each side or until done.

Nutty Burgers

GRILLED FLANK STEAK SANGRITA

Makes 6 servings

2½ to 3 pounds beef flank steak
1 teaspoon salt
¼ teaspoon pepper
1 teaspoon dried thyme, crushed
¼ cup orange juice concentrate, thawed

3 tablespoons vegetable oil
Fruity Wine Sauce (recipe follows)

Lightly score steak and rub with salt, pepper and thyme. Combine orange juice concentrate and oil; pour over steak. Marinate at room temperature 30 minutes. Drain meat; reserve marinade. Grill steak, on covered grill, over medium-hot **Kingsford® briquets** 8 to 10 minutes on each side, turning once and basting often with marinade until done. Cut meat across grain into thin, (slanting) slices. Serve with Fruity Wine Sauce.

FRUITY WINE SAUCE

¾ cup chopped green onion with tops
1½ cups red wine
1 orange, thinly sliced

1 lime, thinly sliced
1 apple, thinly sliced
½ cup butter or margarine
2 tablespoons chopped parsley

Combine onion, red wine and fruit in small saucepan; bring to boil. Add butter and parsley; cook and stir until butter is melted and sauce is hot. Ladle over beef and serve.

SPICY COUNTRY RIBS

Makes 6 servings

1 medium onion, finely chopped
3 cloves garlic, crushed
2 tablespoons vegetable oil
1 can (15 ounces) tomato sauce
½ cup red wine
¼ cup packed brown sugar
¾ teaspoon salt

½ teaspoon dry mustard
½ teaspoon chili powder
½ teaspoon hot pepper sauce
⅛ teaspoon black pepper
5 pounds country-style spare ribs

Sauté onion and garlic in oil until onion is transparent. Stir in remaining ingredients, except spare ribs. Heat mixture to boiling. Reduce heat and simmer, covered, 20 minutes. Trim any excess fat from ribs. Arrange ribs in large shallow glass casserole. Cover with plastic wrap, vented. Microwave on 50% power 20 minutes. Rearrange ribs once. Remove from oven. Brush ribs with sauce. Lightly oil grid. Grill ribs, on covered grill, over medium-hot **Kingsford® briquets**, turning and basting often, 30 minutes or until meat near the bone loses its pink color.

Charcoal Beef Kabobs

CHARCOAL BEEF KABOBS

Makes 4 servings

½ cup vegetable oil
¼ cup lemon juice
1½ tablespoons (½ package)
    Hidden Valley Ranch®
    Original Ranch® Salad
    Dressing Mix

2 pounds beef, cut into 1-inch
    cubes
2 medium green peppers, cut
    into 1-inch squares
1 medium onion, cut into wedges
    Cherry tomatoes

Combine oil, lemon juice and dry salad dressing mix. Pour over beef cubes
in shallow dish. Cover and refrigerate 1 hour or longer. Thread beef cubes,
green peppers and onion alternately onto skewers. Grill kabobs, on
uncovered grill, over medium-hot **Kingsford® briquets** 15 minutes, brushing
often with marinade and turning to brown all sides. Add cherry tomatoes to
ends of skewers just a few minutes before serving.

Grilled Porterhouse Steaks with Italian-Style Vegetables

GRILLED PORTERHOUSE STEAKS WITH ITALIAN-STYLE VEGETABLES

Makes 4 servings

2 porterhouse steaks, cut 1 to
    1½ inches thick (about
    2 pounds)
2 cloves garlic, minced, divided
1½ teaspoons dried basil leaves,
    divided
½ teaspoon coarse ground black
    pepper
1 tablespoon olive oil

1 large zucchini, cut into ½-inch
    pieces
1 small onion, cut into thin
    wedges
1¼ cups sliced mushrooms
¼ teaspoon salt
6 cherry tomatoes, cut into
    halves

Season each steak with 1 clove garlic, ¾ teaspoon basil and the pepper. Grill steaks, on uncovered grill, over medium-hot **Kingsford®** briquets, turning once. Steaks cut 1 inch thick require about 16 minutes for rare; 20 minutes for medium. Steaks cut 1½ inches thick require about 22 minutes

(continued)

for rare; 30 minutes for medium. After turning steaks, heat oil in frying pan on grid over coals. Add remaining clove garlic, zucchini and onion and sauté 4 to 5 minutes. Add mushrooms, salt and remaining ¾ teaspoon basil. Continue cooking 2 minutes, stirring frequently. Add tomatoes; heat through. Serve vegetables with steaks.

Favorite recipe from **National Live Stock & Meat Board**

ORANGE FLAVORED GRILLED BEEF

Makes 4 servings

1 tablespoon grated orange peel
2 tablespoons brown sugar
2 tablespoons cider vinegar
3 tablespoons soy sauce
½ teaspoon pepper
½ teaspoon chili powder

1 garlic clove, minced
1 teaspoon minced fresh ginger
1 orange, peeled and quartered
2 pounds beef round tip roast,
    cut into 3-inch cubes

Combine all ingredients, except beef, in bowl. Add beef cubes; toss to coat with marinade. Cover and refrigerate 8 hours or overnight. Drain meat cubes; reserve marinade. Grill beef cubes, on covered grill, over medium-hot **Kingsford®** briquets 3 minutes. Turn beef cubes, brush with marinade and cook 5 minutes longer or until done.

TEXAS-STYLE STEAK ON HOT BREAD

Makes 4 to 6 servings

½ cup olive or vegetable oil
¼ cup lime juice
¼ cup red wine vinegar
1 medium onion, finely chopped
1 large clove garlic, minced
¼ teaspoon ground cumin
1 teaspoon chili powder

½ teaspoon salt
1½ pounds skirt or flank steak
1 round loaf French or sourdough
    bread
1 cup Mexican-style salsa
1 cup guacamole

Combine all ingredients, except steak, bread, salsa and guacamole, in large glass dish. Pound steak to ¼ inch thickness. Place steak in marinade; turn to coat. Cover and refrigerate overnight or several hours, turning several times. Drain steak; discard marinade. Grill steak, on covered grill, over medium-hot **Kingsford® with Mesquite charcoal briquets** 4 to 8 minutes on each side, or until done. Cut bread into 1-inch slices and toast on grill. Heat salsa. Arrange steak, sliced into ¾-inch diagonal strips, on toasted bread. Top with hot salsa and guacamole.

Giant Cheese Burgers

GIANT CHEESE BURGERS

Makes 6 servings

1½ cups shredded Monterey Jack
    cheese (about 8 ounces)
1 can (2¼ ounces) chopped
    black olives
⅛ teaspoon red pepper sauce
1¾ pounds ground beef

¼ cup finely chopped onion
1 teaspoon salt
½ teaspoon black pepper
6 whole wheat hamburger buns
    Butter or margarine, melted

Combine cheese, olives and red pepper sauce; mix well. Divide mixture
evenly and shape into 6 balls. Mix ground beef with onion, salt and pepper;
shape into 12 thin patties. Place a cheese ball in center of 6 patties and top
each with a second patty. Seal edges of each patty to enclose cheese ball.
Lightly oil grid. Grill patties, on covered grill, over medium-hot **Kingsford®
briquets** 5 to 6 minutes on each side or until done.

Split buns, brush with butter and place cut-side down on grill to heat
through. Serve Cheese Burgers on buns.

BARBECUED BUTTERFLIED EYE ROUND ROAST

Makes 4 to 6 servings

1 can (12 ounces) beer
¼ cup vegetable oil
¼ cup cider vinegar
1 medium onion, chopped
2 large cloves garlic, minced

½ teaspoon pepper
1 beef eye round roast (about 3 pounds), butterflied
1 cup K.C. Masterpiece® Barbecue Sauce

Combine beer, oil, vinegar, onion, garlic and pepper in bowl. Place roast in large glass dish. Pour marinade over beef; turn to coat. Cover and refrigerate overnight, turning occasionally. Remove roast from marinade; discard marinade. Grill beef, on covered grill, over medium-hot **Kingsford® briquets** 25 minutes, turning and basting often with barbecue sauce. Season with salt, if desired. Carve roast into thin slices. Heat remaining barbecue sauce and serve with beef slices.

GRILLED STEAK WITH HOT SWEET ONIONS

Makes 4 servings

3 large onions, cut into ¼-inch thick slices
2 tablespoons honey
½ teaspoon dry mustard
½ teaspoon salt

½ teaspoon paprika
½ teaspoon pepper
4 beef loin T-bone or porterhouse steaks, cut 1 inch thick (8 ounces each)

Arrange sliced onions on large square of heavy-duty foil. Mix honey and mustard; drizzle over onions. Sprinkle with salt, paprika and pepper. Fold foil loosely around onions and seal edges tightly. Grill packet, on covered grill, over medium-hot **Kingsford® with Mesquite charcoal briquets** 20 minutes or until onions are tender; turn once. Slash any fat around edge of steaks about every 4 inches. About 5 minutes after onions start to grill, place steaks on grill with onion packet. Grill 8 to 10 minutes on each side for medium-rare or to desired doneness. Serve onions on top of each steak.

BACK RIBS

Makes 4 servings

4 pounds beef back ribs
 Hoisin Barbecue Sauce (recipe
 follows) or

Pantry Barbecue Sauce (recipe
 follows)

Grill ribs, on uncovered grill, over medium-hot **Match light®** charcoal **briquets** 30 minutes or until almost done; turn every 10 minutes. During last 10 to 15 minutes of cooking, brush ribs generously with either Hoisin Barbecue Sauce or Pantry Barbecue Sauce.

HOISIN BARBECUE SAUCE

Makes 1 cup

Combine ½ cup hoisin sauce, 2 tablespoons white wine, 2 tablespoons vegetable oil, 2 teaspoons minced fresh ginger and 2 cloves minced garlic; mix well.

PANTRY BARBECUE SAUCE

Makes 1 cup

Combine ¾ cup catsup, ¼ cup firmly packed brown sugar, 2 tablespoons soy sauce, 1 tablespoon cider vinegar, ¼ teaspoon ground ginger, ¼ teaspoon hot pepper sauce and 1 medium clove minced garlic in small bowl; mix well.

PEPPER STUFFED FLANK STEAK

Makes 6 to 8 servings

2 beef flank steaks (1 pound
 each)
¼ teaspoon garlic powder
¼ teaspoon black pepper
1 green pepper, cut into strips
1 red pepper, cut into strips
1 onion, cut into thin slices
1 can (15 ounces) tomato sauce

½ cup finely chopped onion
¼ cup soy sauce
1 tablespoon sugar
1 teaspoon dry mustard
1 teaspoon garlic powder
⅛ teaspoon cayenne pepper
¼ cup vegetable oil

Pound each steak with mallet to ¼ inch thickness. Sprinkle steaks with garlic powder and pepper. Arrange green and red pepper strips horizontally on steaks. Cover with onion slices. Starting at narrow end of each steak, roll up jelly-roll fashion; tie with string. Set aside. Combine remaining ingredients, except oil, in large jar with screw top. Shake to blend. Brush all sides of steaks with oil. Lightly oil grid. Grill steaks, on covered grill, 4 to 6 inches above hot **Kingsford®** **briquets** about 30 minutes, turning often, until done. Brush steaks with tomato-soy mixture during last 10 minutes of grilling.

Barbecued Beef Tip Roast

BARBECUED BEEF TIP ROAST

Makes 8 to 10 servings

1 tablespoon Italian seasoning	½ teaspoon cayenne pepper
1 teaspoon garlic salt	1 beef tip roast (6 to 8 pounds)

Combine Italian seasoning, garlic salt and cayenne pepper; rub evenly over roast. Arrange medium-hot **Kingsford® briquets** around drip pan. Place roast over drip pan. Insert meat thermometer so bulb is centered in thickest part (make certain bulb does not rest in fat). Partially close bottom dampers, if necessary, to control heat. Cover grill (leaving top damper open) and cook until meat thermometer registers 140°F for rare; 160°F for medium (allow 30 to 35 minutes per pound). For easier carving, allow roast to "set" in a warm place 15 to 20 minutes after removal from grill. (Since roast usually continues to cook after removal from grill, it is best to remove it about 5°F below temperature desired.)

*Favorite recipe from **Weber Grills** and **Beef Industry Council***

POULTRY

CHICKEN FAJITAS

Makes 6 servings

½ cup vegetable oil
¼ cup red wine vinegar
⅓ cup lime juice
¼ cup finely chopped onion
2 cloves garlic, minced
1 teaspoon sugar
1 teaspoon dried oregano
½ teaspoon salt
½ teaspoon pepper

¼ teaspoon ground cumin
3 whole chicken breasts, halved,
   skinned and boned
Flour tortillas
Chopped tomatoes
Chopped onion
Sliced avocado
Salsa

Combine first 10 ingredients in shallow glass dish; mix well. Add chicken breasts to marinade; turn to coat. Cover and refrigerate chicken 4 hours, turning occasionally. Drain chicken; reserve marinade. Grill chicken, on covered grill, over medium-hot **Kingsford® briquets** 8 minutes; turn and continue grilling 5 to 7 minutes or until cooked through.

While chicken is grilling, wrap tortillas in heavy-duty foil and place on edge of grill. Heat about 15 minutes, turning packet over once. Slice chicken breasts into thin slices. Place slices of chicken and garnishes in warm flour tortillas and roll up.

*Favorite recipe from **Weber Grills***

Chicken Fajitas

Barbecued Turkey

BARBECUED TURKEY

Makes 8 to 10 servings

**1 turkey (9 to 13 pounds), fresh
   or thawed**

**Oil
Salt and pepper**

Remove neck and giblets from turkey. Rinse turkey with cold water; drain and pat dry with paper toweling. Rub outer surface with oil and generously season inside and out with salt and pepper. Pull skin over neck and secure with a skewer. Fold wings behind back and tie legs and tail together with kitchen twine. Insert meat thermometer into center of thickest part of thigh, not touching bone. Arrange medium-hot **Kingsford®** **briquets** around large drip pan. Position turkey directly above drip pan. Cover grill and cook turkey 11 to 13 minutes per pound or until internal temperature reaches 185°F. Add more briquets as necessary, following guidelines for indirect cooking (page 4) for number of briquets needed.

Favorite recipe from **Weber Grills**

CHICKEN KYOTO

Makes 4 to 6 servings

1 cup apple cider
½ cup soy sauce
½ cup vegetable oil
¼ cup sugar

2 teaspoons ground ginger
1 broiler-fryer chicken (2 to
 3 pounds), quartered

In small saucepan, combine all ingredients, except chicken. Simmer over medium heat 5 to 8 minutes or until sugar is dissolved; cool slightly. Place chicken in shallow glass dish. Pour marinade over chicken; cover and refrigerate about 6 hours. Drain chicken; reserve marinade. Grill chicken, on uncovered grill, over medium-hot **Kingsford® briquets** 15 to 20 minutes on each side, basting often with marinade, until fork-tender.

BARBECUED GLAZED CHICKEN

Makes 4 servings

1 jar (16 ounces) orange
 marmalade
⅓ cup soy sauce
¼ cup cider vinegar
2 cloves garlic, crushed

1 broiler-fryer chicken (2 to
 3 pounds), quartered
¼ cup vegetable oil
 Salt and pepper

Combine orange marmalade, soy sauce, vinegar and garlic. Brush both sides of chicken with oil; sprinkle with salt and pepper. Lightly oil grid. Grill chicken skin-side up, on uncovered grill, over medium-hot **Kingsford® briquets** about 45 minutes, turning often, until fork-tender. During last 20 minutes of grilling, brush chicken with marmalade sauce.

GRILLED LEMON CHICKEN

Makes 4 servings

¼ cup fresh lemon juice
1 tablespoon minced onion
1 teaspoon grated lemon peel
1 teaspoon salt
½ teaspoon dried tarragon,
 crushed

½ teaspoon paprika
4 to 5 drops hot pepper sauce
1 broiler-fryer chicken (2 to
 3 pounds), quartered

Combine all ingredients, except chicken. Arrange chicken in shallow glass dish. Pour marinade over chicken; cover and refrigerate 2 to 4 hours. Drain chicken; reserve marinade. Lightly oil grid. Grill chicken, on covered grill, over medium-hot **Kingsford® briquets** 15 to 20 minutes on each side, basting often with marinade, until fork-tender.

TURKEY FILLETS IN SPICY CILANTRO MARINADE

Makes 4 servings

1 cup chopped onion
1 large tomato, quartered
⅓ cup soy sauce
¼ cup chopped green pepper
3 tablespoons vegetable oil

2 tablespoons cilantro or parsley
3 tablespoons lime juice
2 cloves garlic
¾ teaspoon black pepper
4 turkey breast fillets

Place all ingredients, except turkey, in blender; blend 30 seconds. Pour into large plastic bag; add turkey fillets. Close bag securely. Place bag in large bowl and refrigerate 4 hours, turning bag occasionally. Drain turkey fillets; reserve marinade. Grill turkey, on uncovered grill, about 6 inches above hot **Kingsford® briquets** 5 minutes on each side, brushing often with marinade, until tender.

GRILLED STUFFED CHICKEN BREASTS

Makes 6 servings

6 chicken breast halves, skinned
and boned
6 tablespoons butter or
margarine
3 tablespoons Dijon-style
mustard

6 slices cooked ham
1 cup shredded Swiss cheese
(about 4 ounces)
3 tablespoons vegetable oil
1 tablespoon honey
Salt and pepper

Pound chicken breasts to ¼ inch thickness. Blend butter with 2 tablespoons mustard; spread over one side of each chicken breast. Cut one ham slice to fit each chicken piece; top with shredded cheese. Roll chicken pieces and skewer each to enclose ham and cheese. Mix remaining 1 tablespoon mustard with oil and honey; brush all sides of each roll. Grill chicken, on covered grill, over medium-hot **Kingsford® with Mesquite charcoal briquets** 25 to 35 minutes, basting often with mustard-honey mixture, until chicken is tender.

Grilled and Glazed Game Hens

GRILLED AND GLAZED GAME HENS

Makes 4 to 6 servings

½ cup K.C. Masterpiece®
    Barbecue Sauce
¼ cup dry sherry
3 tablespoons frozen orange
    juice concentrate, thawed

4 Cornish game hens (about
    1½ pounds each)

In saucepan, combine barbecue sauce, sherry and juice concentrate. Bring to boil; simmer 10 minutes. Remove from heat; cool. Pat game hen cavities dry with paper toweling; brush with sauce. Grill hens, on covered grill, over medium-hot **Kingsford® briquets** 40 to 50 minutes, turning once, until fork-tender. Baste with sauce during last 10 minutes of grilling. Remove from grill; brush generously with additional sauce.

Kansas City Style Barbecued Chicken Legs

KANSAS CITY STYLE BARBECUED CHICKEN LEGS

Makes 6 servings

½ cup butter or margarine, softened
⅓ cup finely chopped parsley
2 cloves garlic, minced
2¾ to 3 pounds chicken legs (about 12 legs)

3 tablespoons olive or vegetable oil
¾ cup K.C. Masterpiece® Barbecue Sauce

Blend butter, parsley and garlic in small bowl. Rinse chicken legs with cold water; pat dry with paper toweling. Starting at thick end of each leg, work finger between skin and meat to form a pocket. Insert about 2 teaspoons parsley-butter into pocket; massage outer skin to spread filling. Rub completed legs with oil. Lightly oil grid. Grill chicken, on covered grill, over medium-hot **Kingsford® briquets** about 45 minutes or until fork-tender. Turn and baste occasionally with remaining oil. About 15 minutes before chicken is cooked, baste thoroughly with barbecue sauce. Baste once more before serving. Serve with additional warmed barbecue sauce, if desired.

GRILLED TURKEY WITH VEGETABLE PIZZAZZ

Makes 6 servings

1½ pounds turkey breast, cut into
    2-inch pieces
2 medium zucchini, cut into
    1-inch chunks
12 large mushrooms
1 medium red pepper, cut into
    1½-inch pieces

12 jumbo pimiento-stuffed olives
1 tablespoon vegetable oil
1 cup pizza sauce
1 tablespoon dried basil

Thread turkey, zucchini, mushrooms, pepper and olives alternately on skewers; brush thoroughly with oil. Mix pizza sauce and basil; reserve. Grill kabobs, on uncovered grill, over medium-hot **Match light® charcoal briquets** about 10 minutes, turning occasionally. Baste with pizza sauce and continue to grill about 15 minutes, basting and turning 2 to 3 times, until turkey is tender and vegetables are cooked.

SESAME GRILLED CHICKEN

Makes 4 servings

½ cup white wine
⅓ cup white vinegar
1 tablespoon sesame oil
⅓ cup vegetable oil
2 cloves garlic, sliced
1 tablespoon chopped fresh
    ginger

2 sprigs fresh thyme or
    ¼ teaspoon dried thyme
1 tablespoon sesame seeds
1 broiler-fryer chicken (2 to
    3 pounds), quartered

Combine all ingredients, except chicken. Rinse chicken with cold water and pat dry with paper toweling. Arrange chicken in glass baking dish. Pour marinade over chicken. Cover and marinate about 3 hours at room temperature or up to 24 hours in refrigerator. Remove chicken; reserve marinade. Grill chicken quarters skin-side down, on covered grill, over medium-hot **Kingsford® briquets** 15 to 20 minutes, brushing often with marinade. Turn and cook about 20 minutes longer, brushing often with marinade, until chicken is fork-tender.

BARBECUED CHICKEN

Makes 4 to 5 servings

¼ cup catsup
2 tablespoons vinegar
1 cup chicken broth
2 tablespoons Worcestershire
  sauce
2 tablespoons finely chopped
  onion

1 teaspoon dry mustard
½ teaspoon garlic salt
½ teaspoon salt
¼ teaspoon pepper
1 broiler-fryer chicken (2 to
  3 pounds), quartered

Combine all ingredients, except chicken, in small saucepan. Bring to boil;
cool slightly. Place chicken in shallow glass dish. Pour warm sauce over
chicken; cover and refrigerate at least 2 hours. Grill chicken skin-side up, on
uncovered grill, over hot **Kingsford®** briquets 40 to 55 minutes, basting often
with marinade and turning frequently, until chicken is fork-tender.

GRILLED GAME HENS, TEXAS-STYLE

Makes 4 servings

1 can (8 ounces) tomato sauce
¼ cup vegetable oil
1½ teaspoons chili powder
1 teaspoon paprika

¼ teaspoon garlic powder
¼ teaspoon cayenne pepper
4 Cornish game hens (1 to
  1½ pounds each), halved

Combine all ingredients, except game hens, in small bowl. Brush hens
generously with tomato mixture. Grill hens, on covered grill, over medium-
hot **Kingsford® with Mesquite charcoal briquets** 40 to 50 minutes, brushing
several times with tomato mixture, until fork-tender.

LEMON HERBED CHICKEN

Makes 6 servings

½ cup butter or margarine
½ cup vegetable oil
⅓ cup lemon juice
2 tablespoons finely chopped
  parsley
2 tablespoons garlic salt

1 teaspoon dried rosemary
1 teaspoon dried summer savory,
  crushed
½ teaspoon dried thyme
¼ teaspoon pepper
6 chicken breasts

Combine all ingredients, except chicken, in saucepan. Heat until butter
melts. Arrange chicken in shallow glass dish and brush with sauce 10 to 15
minutes before cooking. Lightly oil grid. Grill chicken skin-side up, on
uncovered grill, over medium-hot **Kingsford®** briquets 45 to 60 minutes,
turning and basting with sauce every 10 minutes, until fork-tender.

Oriental Grilled Chicken

ORIENTAL GRILLED CHICKEN

Makes 4 servings

2 tablespoons prepared mustard
¼ cup soy sauce
4 teaspoons honey
1 tablespoon lemon juice

¼ teaspoon ground ginger
1 broiler-fryer chicken (2 to
    3 pounds), quartered*

In medium bowl, combine mustard and soy sauce. Gradually stir in honey; then add lemon juice and ginger. Place chicken in glass dish. Pour marinade over chicken; cover and refrigerate about 1 hour. Grill chicken skin-side up, on covered grill, over medium-hot **Kingsford®** **briquets** about 45 minutes to 1 hour, until fork-tender. Baste generously with sauce during last 15 minutes of grilling.

*16 broiler-fryer chicken wings may be used instead of chicken quarters. Cut grilling time to about 30 minutes.

*Favorite recipe from **National Broiler Council***

KINGSFORD®

PORK & LAMB

BUTTERFLIED LEG OF LAMB WITH ORANGE SAUCE

10 to 12 servings

3½ to 4 pound butterflied leg of lamb
⅔ cup orange juice
½ cup orange marmalade
1 tablespoon butter or margarine

½ teaspoon grated fresh ginger
¼ teaspoon dry mustard
2 tablespoons lemon juice
1 tablespoon cornstarch

Thread 2 long metal skewers through butterflied leg of lamb to secure and facilitate turning roast. Grill lamb, on covered grill, over medium-hot **Kingsford® briquets** to desired doneness. Allow 40 to 60 minutes total cooking time.

Meanwhile, combine orange juice, marmalade, butter, ginger and mustard in small saucepan. Cook over medium-low heat until marmalade is melted, stirring occasionally. Combine lemon juice and cornstarch; stir into orange juice mixture and cook until thickened. Remove from heat; reserve. Turn leg several times during cooking, brushing with ⅓ cup reserved sauce during last 10 minutes of cooking. Remove skewers and separate leg into three sections along natural seams. Carve each section across the grain into thin slices. Serve remaining sauce with carved lamb.

Favorite recipe from **National Live Stock & Meat Board**

Butterflied Leg of Lamb with Orange Sauce

ALL-AMERICAN PORK RIBS

Makes 4 servings

½ teaspoon salt
3 pounds pork loin back ribs
1 small onion, coarsely chopped
2 tablespoons water
⅔ cup catsup
⅔ cup chili sauce

2 tablespoons lemon juice
½ teaspoon dry mustard
¼ teaspoon ground red pepper
¼ teaspoon paprika
¼ teaspoon Worcestershire
   sauce

Rub salt over surface of pork. Grill ribs, on covered grill, over medium to low **Kingsford® briquets** 45 minutes to 1 hour or until done, turning occasionally.

Meanwhile, cook onion in water in medium saucepan 3 to 4 minutes. Add remaining ingredients and cook slowly 15 minutes. Brush both sides of ribs with sauce during last 10 minutes of cooking. Serve remaining sauce with ribs.

Note: Recipe may be doubled.

*Favorite recipe from **National Live Stock & Meat Board***

GRILLED LAMB & VEGETABLE KABOBS

Makes 4 servings

⅔ cup dry sherry
3 tablespoons olive or vegetable
   oil
1 teaspoon salt
1 teaspoon Worcestershire
   sauce
¼ teaspoon black pepper
¼ teaspoon dried oregano
¼ teaspoon dried rosemary

¼ teaspoon dried thyme
1¼ to 1½ pounds boneless lamb
   cubes, cut into 1¼-inch
   pieces
8 small white onions
1 small red pepper, cut into
   8 pieces
8 medium fresh whole
   mushrooms

Combine sherry, oil, salt, Worcestershire sauce, pepper, oregano, rosemary and thyme. Place lamb cubes and marinade in plastic bag. Tie bag securely and refrigerate 2 hours.

Meanwhile, cook onions in boiling water to cover 8 minutes. Blanch red pepper pieces 2 minutes. Drain lamb cubes; reserve marinade. Thread 4 lamb cubes, 2 mushrooms, 2 onions and 2 red pepper pieces alternately on each of four 12-inch skewers. Brush both sides of kabobs with reserved marinade. Grill kabobs, on uncovered grill, over medium-hot **Kingsford® briquets** 8 to 12 minutes or to desired doneness.

*Favorite recipe from **National Live Stock & Meat Board***

Sweet & Sour Pork Loin

SWEET & SOUR PORK LOIN

Makes 4 servings

½ cup chicken broth or water
½ cup catsup
2 tablespoons brown sugar
2 tablespoons cider vinegar
2 tablespoons Worcestershire
    sauce

1 clove garlic, crushed
⅛ teaspoon ground red pepper
½ teaspoon salt
¼ teaspoon black pepper
2 pounds boneless pork roast,
    cut into 4 pieces

Combine all ingredients, except roast, in saucepan. Bring to boil. Arrange pork pieces in shallow glass dish and cover with sweet and sour mixture. Cover and refrigerate overnight. Drain pork; reserve sweet and sour mixture. Grill pork, on uncovered grill, over medium-hot **Match light**® **charcoal briquets** 20 to 25 minutes or until cooked, turning 3 to 4 times and basting often with sweet and sour mixture.

GRILLED SMOKED SAUSAGE

Makes 6 servings

1 cup apricot or pineapple
    preserves

1 tablespoon lemon juice
1½ pounds smoked sausage

Heat preserves and strain; reserve fruit pieces. Combine strained preserve liquid with lemon juice. Grill whole sausage, on uncovered grill, over low **Kingsford**® **briquets** 5 minutes. Brush with glaze; continue to grill and glaze sausage about 5 minutes longer, turning occasionally. Garnish with fruit pieces.

PEACH PORK HOT

Makes 6 to 8 servings

6 to 7 pound boneless pork
 tenderloin roast
2 cups catsup
½ cup soy sauce
½ cup vegetable oil
½ cup peach jam
½ cup hot jalapeño jelly

¼ teaspoon pepper
½ teaspoon grated fresh ginger
1 clove garlic, crushed
½ teaspoon onion powder
¼ teaspoon Hungarian hot
 paprika

Grill pork loin, on uncovered grill, over medium-hot **Kingsford®** briquets about 1½ to 2 hours or until done. Combine remaining ingredients to make sauce. Baste pork loin with sauce during last 20 minutes of grilling.

GRILLED SAUSAGE WITH APPLES & ONIONS

Makes 4 servings

1 pound smoked sausage, cut
 into 1-inch chunks
2 small apples, cored and
 quartered

2 small onions, quartered
2 tablespoons apple jelly
1 tablespoon butter or margarine

Thread sausage, apples and onions alternately on 4 skewers. Combine jelly and butter; heat until melted. Brush butter mixture on sausage, apples and onions. Grill kabobs, on uncovered grill, over medium-hot **Match light®** **charcoal briquets** 10 to 15 minutes or until cooked, basting with butter mixture and turning often.

SATAY PORK

Makes 4 to 6 servings

3 pounds boneless lean pork, cut
 into ½-inch cubes
½ cup peanut or vegetable oil
¼ cup soy sauce
2 tablespoons chopped peanuts
1 tablespoon Worcestershire
 sauce

1 tablespoon chopped onion
2 cloves garlic, crushed
2 teaspoons brown sugar
¼ teaspoon curry powder
⅛ teaspoon coriander

Place pork in shallow glass dish. Combine remaining ingredients and pour over pork. Cover and refrigerate 1 to 2 hours; stir occasionally. Remove meat from refrigerator at least 30 minutes before cooking. Drain pork; reserve marinade. Thread meat onto skewers; grill and baste, on uncovered grill, over hot **Kingsford®** **briquets** about 5 to 6 minutes or until done.

Spicy Lamb Burgers

SPICY LAMB BURGERS

Makes 6 servings

¼ cup chopped onion
1 teaspoon curry powder
1 tablespoon butter or margarine,
    melted
¼ cup finely chopped almonds
¼ cup crushed pineapple,
    drained

1½ pounds ground lamb
½ cup dry bread crumbs
2 eggs
⅛ teaspoon pepper
6 pita breads

Cook onion and curry powder in butter until onion is tender. Stir in almonds and crushed pineapple. Mix thoroughly with lamb, bread crumbs, eggs and pepper. Shape meat mixture into 6 patties. Grill patties, on uncovered grill, over medium-hot **Match light® charcoal briquets** about 5 minutes on each side, or until done. Grill pita breads on edge of grill. Serve lamb burgers in pita breads.

Apricot-Glazed Lamb Chops

APRICOT-GLAZED LAMB CHOPS

Makes 4 to 5 servings

⅓ cup apricot jam
1 tablespoon white vinegar
1 teaspoon Dijon-style mustard
½ teaspoon dried rosemary
½ teaspoon salt

1 clove garlic, minced
¼ teaspoon pepper
4 lamb shoulder or blade chops,
   cut ¾ inch thick

Combine apricot jam, vinegar, mustard, rosemary, salt, garlic and pepper in small saucepan; cook slowly, stirring, until melted. Grill lamb chops, on uncovered grill, over medium-hot **Kingsford® briquets** 14 to 16 minutes for medium, turning once. Brush both sides with glaze several times during grilling.

*Favorite recipe from **National Live Stock & Meat Board***

GRILLED HAM SANDWICHES

Makes 6 servings

1 pound fully cooked ham
1 cup catsup
⅓ cup butter or margarine, melted
1½ tablespoons Worcestershire
    sauce

1½ tablespoons prepared mustard
1 teaspoon onion salt
6 buttered hot dog buns

Cut ham lengthwise into 6 slices. Combine catsup, butter, Worcestershire sauce, mustard and onion salt in small saucepan; heat over low heat until mixture simmers. Remove sauce from heat; cool slightly.

Coat ham slices with sauce. Grill coated meat, on uncovered grill, over medium-hot **Match light® charcoal briquets** 3 to 4 minutes on each side or until meat is browned and hot. Serve sliced ham in hot dog buns.

CIDER GLAZED PORK ROAST

Makes 6 servings

1 pork loin roast (4 to 5 pounds),
    boned and tied
½ cup apple cider

¼ cup Dijon-style mustard
¼ cup vegetable oil
¼ cup soy sauce

Insert meat thermometer in center of thickest part of roast. Arrange medium-hot **Kingsford® briquets** around drip pan. Place roast over drip pan. Cover grill and cook 2½ to 3 hours, adding more briquets as necessary. Combine apple cider, mustard, oil and soy sauce. Brush roast with basting sauce 3 or 4 times during last 30 minutes of cooking.

BASQUE LAMB

Makes 4 to 6 servings

4 lemons, juiced
1 cup dry sherry
½ cup olive or vegetable oil
1 clove garlic, crushed
1 lamb shoulder (3 pounds),
    boned

1 bunch chives, chopped
1 clove garlic, diced
1 bunch parsley, chopped
Salt and pepper

Mix lemon juice, sherry, oil and crushed garlic. Let stand 1 hour. Season inside of lamb shoulder by sprinkling with an even layer of chives, garlic and parsley. Roll shoulder and secure with string. Season with salt and pepper. Arrange medium-hot **Kingsford® briquets** around drip pan. Fill pan with water. Place lamb shoulder on grill over drip pan. Add hickory chips to briquets, if desired. Cover grill and cook 1 to 1½ hours, basting often with lemon juice mixture. Remove lamb from grill; let stand 15 minutes before serving. Carve into 1-inch thick slices.

BARBECUED ALASKA SALMON

Makes 12 to 16 servings

2 whole Alaska salmon fillets
   (about 1½ pounds *each*)
Salt and pepper
½ cup butter or margarine, melted

¼ cup fresh lemon juice
4 teaspoons grated onion
1 teaspoon grated lemon peel
½ teaspoon hot pepper sauce

Rinse salmon fillets with cold water; pat dry with paper toweling. Sprinkle both sides of each fillet with salt and pepper. Combine remaining ingredients; brush both sides of fillets with butter mixture. Place each fillet, skin-side down, on sheet of well-oiled heavy-duty foil. Grill salmon, on uncovered grill, over hot **Kingsford®** **briquets** 10 minutes per inch of thickness measured at its thickest part, or until salmon flakes easily when tested with fork. Baste often with butter mixture.

Favorite recipe from **Alaska Seafood Marketing Institute, Salmon Division**

ORIENTAL BARBECUED SCALLOPS

Makes 6 to 8 servings

½ cup soy sauce
1 tablespoon sugar
2 teaspoons lemon juice
1 teaspoon sesame oil

1 clove garlic, crushed
2 tablespoons white wine
3 to 4 pounds large sea scallops

Mix all ingredients, except scallops, in large bowl. Add scallops; cover and refrigerate 1 hour. Thread scallops on skewers. Grill scallops, on uncovered grill, over medium-hot **Kingsford®** **briquets** 10 minutes, turning and brushing with marinade, until scallops turn opaque.

Barbecued Alaska Salmon and Potatoes Roasted in Coals (see page 93)

GRILLED TROUT WITH TWO SAUCES

Makes 4 servings

4 whole, cleaned trout or other small whole fish (about 12 ounces *each*)
Walnut Butter Sauce (recipe follows) or

Tarragon Cream Sauce (recipe follows)

Grill fish on well-oiled grid or in well-oiled wire grill basket, on covered grill, over medium-hot **Kingsford® with Mesquite charcoal briquets** 3 to 5 minutes or until fish flakes easily when tested with fork; turn once. Serve with Walnut Butter Sauce or Tarragon Cream Sauce.

WALNUT BUTTER SAUCE

½ cup chopped walnuts
½ cup butter or margarine

3 tablespoons Madeira wine

Sauté walnuts in 2 tablespoons butter until golden and fragrant. Reduce heat and add remaining 6 tablespoons butter; stir until melted. Stir in Madeira. Serve warm.

TARRAGON CREAM SAUCE

¼ cup olive or vegetable oil
¼ cup whipping cream
1 tablespoon red wine vinegar
1 tablespoon finely chopped parsley

1 egg yolk, beaten
½ teaspoon dried tarragon
¼ teaspoon pepper
1 small clove garlic, minced

Combine all ingredients in bowl; mix well with wire whip. Serve cool.

CANTONESE GRILLED SHRIMP

Makes 4 to 6 servings

2 pounds medium shrimp, shelled and deveined
1 cup soy sauce
½ cup dry white or red wine
2 tablespoons vegetable oil
4 green onions, finely chopped

2 tablespoons grated fresh ginger
2 tablespoons brown sugar
2 teaspoons crushed red pepper
2 teaspoons sesame seeds

Place shrimp in shallow glass dish. Combine remaining ingredients; pour over shrimp. Cover and refrigerate at least 2 hours or overnight, stirring occasionally. Thread shrimp onto skewers. Grill shrimp, on covered grill, over medium-hot **Kingsford® briquets** 6 to 8 minutes, basting constantly with marinade, until shrimp turn pink.

SALMON STEAKS IN ORANGE-HONEY MARINADE

Makes 4 servings

⅓ cup orange juice
⅓ cup soy sauce
3 tablespoons peanut oil
3 tablespoons catsup
1 tablespoon honey

½ teaspoon ground ginger
1 clove garlic, crushed
4 salmon steaks (about 6 ounces each)

In 1-quart measure, mix all ingredients except salmon steaks. Place salmon steaks in shallow glass dish. Pour marinade over salmon steaks; cover and refrigerate 1 hour. Grill salmon, on uncovered grill, 6 inches above hot **Kingsford®** briquets 5 minutes. Carefully turn salmon steaks, brush with marinade and grill 5 minutes longer or until salmon flakes easily when tested with fork.

GRILLED SUMMER FISH

Makes 4 servings

1¼ pounds fish fillets (cod, blue fish, haddock, sole)
1 medium green pepper, coarsely chopped
1 ripe medium tomato, coarsely chopped

¼ cup chopped green onions
1 tablespoon chopped fresh dill
½ teaspoon salt
2 tablespoons lemon juice
1 cup shredded Jarlsberg cheese (about 4 ounces)

Cut piece of heavy-duty foil approximately 18×12 inches; grease lightly. Place fish fillets in center of foil. Combine vegetables; place over fish. Sprinkle with dill and salt; drizzle with lemon juice. Top with Jarlsberg cheese. Fold edges of foil around fish to seal tightly allowing room for heat circulation. Grill packet, on uncovered grill, over hot **Kingsford®** briquets about 25 minutes. Carefully open packet and check to see if fish is cooked. If fillets are still translucent, reseal and cook 5 to 10 minutes longer. (Cooking time will depend upon the thickness of the fish fillets and heat of coals.)

*Favorite recipe from **Norseland Foods***

GRILLED LOBSTER WITH SPICY SAUCE

Makes 4 servings

4 whole, live lobsters (1 to
  1½ pounds each)*
¼ cup dry sherry
3 tablespoons soy sauce
2 to 3 tablespoons sugar
2 teaspoons grated fresh ginger,
  or ½ teaspoon ground ginger

1 teaspoon dried, crushed red
  chili peppers
2 cloves garlic, minced
Butter or margarine

Bring large kettle of water to boil. Plunge lobsters into water. Return water to boil; cover and simmer 3 minutes or just until lobsters turn pink. Remove lobsters; rinse with cold water and drain. Turn lobsters, undersides up, and cut through inner shell of tails to expose meat. For spicy sauce, combine remaining ingredients, except butter. Brush lobsters, shells and meaty undersides with sauce, letting it soak into meat. Grill lobsters, meat-side up, on covered grill, over medium-hot **Kingsford® with Mesquite charcoal briquets** 13 to 15 minutes, basting often with sauce, until meat turns opaque. When lobsters are cooked, make a deep cut lengthwise in center of lobsters' undersides with a sharp, pointed knife. Spread halves enough to remove stomach (near head) and black line. Crack claw shells with hammer. Serve with melted butter and additional spicy sauce.

*2 pounds fresh prawns may be substituted for lobster. Leave shell on and thread onto skewers. Grill as above, reducing cooking time to 5 minutes.

CAJUN FISH

Makes 4 servings

1 cup butter or margarine
2 tablespoons paprika
2 teaspoons popcorn butter salt
2 teaspoons onion powder
2 teaspoons garlic powder
2 teaspoons cayenne pepper

1½ teaspoons white pepper
1½ teaspoons black pepper
1 teaspoon dried thyme
1 teaspoon dried oregano
2 pounds red snapper fillets

Melt butter and set aside. Combine all seasonings. Heat cast iron skillet directly over hot **Match light® charcoal briquets** at least 15 minutes. Dip fillets in butter; sprinkle seasoning mix evenly on both sides of fillets. Place fillets in hot skillet and ladle melted butter over fillets.* Cook about 2 minutes on each side. Serve immediately with melted butter for dipping.

*Note: This method of grilling produces heavy smoke.

Grilled Shrimp in Peanut Sauce

GRILLED SHRIMP IN PEANUT SAUCE

Makes 4 servings

¼ cup creamy peanut butter
¼ cup soy sauce
¼ cup sugar
3 cloves garlic, minced

2 tablespoons vegetable oil
1 tablespoon water
1½ pounds medium shrimp,
    shelled and deveined

Mix peanut butter and 2 tablespoons soy sauce in saucepan. Blend in remaining soy sauce, sugar, garlic, oil and water; heat to dissolve sugar. Thread 4 shrimp to a skewer; brush with peanut sauce. Grill shrimp, on covered grill, over medium-hot **Kingsford® with Mesquite charcoal briquets** 5 to 6 minutes or until shrimp turn pink; turn once. Brush shrimp with peanut sauce before serving.

TUNA WITH LIME & GINGER

Makes 6 servings

3 pounds fresh tuna
½ cup olive or vegetable oil
¼ cup lime juice
1 cup dry white wine

2 cloves garlic, crushed
1 teaspoon grated fresh ginger
6 slices bacon

Cut tuna into 6 steaks, each about 1 inch thick. Remove any skin or bone. Combine remaining ingredients, except bacon. Pour over tuna; cover and refrigerate 2 hours. Remove fish; reserve marinade. Wrap a slice of bacon around each steak and secure with wooden toothpick. Lightly oil grid. Grill fish steaks, on uncovered grill, over medium-hot **Kingsford® briquets** about 10 minutes, basting often with marinade, until fish flakes easily when tested with fork.

Seafood Kabobs

SEAFOOD KABOBS

Makes 6 servings

2 dozen large sea scallops
1 dozen medium shrimp, shelled
and deveined
1 can (8½ ounces) artichoke
hearts, drained

2 red or yellow peppers, cut into
2-inch pieces
¼ cup olive or vegetable oil
¼ cup lime juice

Combine all ingredients in bowl and toss gently; thread scallops, shrimp,
artichoke hearts and peppers alternately onto skewers. Lightly oil grid. Grill
kabobs, on uncovered grill, over low **Kingsford® briquets** 6 to 8 minutes or
until scallops turn opaque. Turn kabobs carefully at least twice during grilling
and brush with marinade. Brush again just before serving.

SWORDFISH WITH WINE-HERB BASTE

Makes 4 servings

½ cup dry white wine
1 tablespoon vegetable oil
1 teaspoon dried rosemary
½ teaspoon salt
1 clove garlic, crushed

½ teaspoon dried oregano
2 pounds swordfish steaks,
   halibut or cod, each about
   1 inch thick

Combine all ingredients, except fish steaks. Arrange fish in shallow glass dish. Pour wine-herb mixture over fish. Cover and refrigerate overnight. Drain steaks; reserve wine-herb mixture. Lightly oil grid. Grill fish steaks, on uncovered grill, over medium-hot **Match light® charcoal briquets** 5 to 8 minutes on each side, basting often with wine-herb mixture, until fish flakes easily when tested with fork.

SESAME COD

Makes 4 servings

1¼ pounds cod or other firm white
   fish
¼ cup orange juice
2 tablespoons catsup
2 tablespoons soy sauce
1 tablespoon lemon juice

¼ teaspoon pepper
1 teaspoon sesame or vegetable
   oil
1 tablespoon brown sugar
1 tablespoon sesame seeds,
   toasted

Rinse fish with cold water; pat dry with paper toweling. Cut fish into 4 equal serving portions. Place fish in single layer in shallow glass dish. Combine orange juice, catsup, soy sauce, lemon juice, pepper, oil and brown sugar; pour over fish. Cover and refrigerate 2 hours, turning once. Remove fish; reserve marinade. Place fish in well-greased hinged wire grill basket; baste with sauce. Grill, on uncovered grill (basted side to fire), about 4 to 6 inches above hot **Kingsford® briquets** 5 to 7 minutes. Baste top with sauce. Turn and cook 4 to 5 minutes longer or until fish flakes easily when tested with fork. Heat remaining sauce; pour over fish. Sprinkle with sesame seeds.

FRUITS & VEGETABLES

GRILLED SHERRIED FRUIT

Makes 6 servings

1 can (8¼ ounces) sliced
   pineapple, drained
2 large oranges, peeled and
   sliced
¼ cup seedless golden raisins

¼ cup dry sherry
3 tablespoons grated orange
   peel
¼ teaspoon nutmeg

Arrange fruit in lightly oiled foil pan. Sprinkle with remaining ingredients.
Cover tightly with foil. Place pan on grill over medium-hot **Kingsford**®
briquets 25 minutes or until fruit is hot.

TEXAS-STYLE CORN & LIMAS

Makes 4 to 6 servings

1 can (17 ounces) whole kernel
   corn, drained
1 can (16 ounces) lima beans,
   drained
¼ cup sliced ripe olives, drained
2 tablespoons finely chopped
   onion

1½ teaspoons seasoned salt
1½ teaspoons chili powder
⅛ teaspoon pepper
3 tablespoons butter or
   margarine

Place corn and lima beans in center of double-thick square of heavy-duty
foil. Sprinkle remaining ingredients, except butter, over corn and limas. Dot
with butter. Fold foil loosely around vegetables and seal. Grill packet over
medium-hot **Kingsford**® **briquets** 15 minutes or until vegetables are tender.
Turn packet several times.

Spicy Quesadillas

SPICY QUESADILLAS

Makes 8 to 10 appetizer servings

½ cup chopped fresh tomatoes
⅓ cup K.C. Masterpiece®
    Barbecue Sauce (Spicy or
    Original)
⅔ cup sliced green onions
2 tablespoons lime or lemon
    juice
1 tablespoon red wine vinegar
1 tablespoon minced jalapeño
    pepper or 2 tablespoons
    diced green chilies

Hot pepper sauce
2 cups shredded Muenster or
    Monterey Jack cheese
8 flour tortillas, about 7 inches in
    diameter
Oil for frying

In small bowl, combine tomatoes, barbecue sauce, 3 tablespoons onions, lime juice, vinegar and pepper. Season to taste with hot pepper sauce. Combine cheese with remaining onions. For each quesadilla, sprinkle about ½ cup cheese-onion mixture over a tortilla. Spoon 2 tablespoons sauce mixture over cheese; top with another tortilla, pressing gently. Fry in skillet in small amount of hot oil until golden and cheese has melted, turning once. Cut into 6 or 8 wedges. Repeat with remaining ingredients. Serve warm with remaining sauce mixture for dipping.

BAKED TOMATOES WITH PEAS AND CARROTS

Makes 6 servings

6 medium tomatoes
1 package (9 ounces) frozen
   peas and carrots, thawed

¼ cup butter or margarine, melted
¼ cup grated Parmesan cheese
   Salt and pepper

Core tomatoes. Scoop out pulp leaving shell. Arrange tomatoes on large piece of heavy-duty foil. Toss thawed peas and carrots with 1 tablespoon melted butter. Spoon vegetables into tomato shells. Drizzle remaining butter over tomatoes. Top with Parmesan cheese and season to taste with salt and pepper. Bring four corners of foil up together into pyramid shape. Fold opening together loosely, allowing room for heat circulation. Grill packet over medium-hot **Kingsford® briquets** 20 minutes or until hot.

CHEDDAR CHEESE PEARS

Makes 6 servings

1 can (29 ounces) pear halves,
   drained, or 3 fresh pears,
   peeled and cut into halves

2 tablespoons fresh lemon juice
2 teaspoons grated lemon peel
½ cup shredded Cheddar cheese

Arrange pears on large square of heavy-duty foil. Sprinkle lemon juice and peel over pears. Fill pear halves with cheese. Fold foil loosely around pears and seal. Grill packet over medium-hot **Kingsford® briquets** 15 minutes or until pears are hot and cheese is soft.

FRESH FRUIT KABOBS

Makes 8 servings

½ cup butter or margarine,
   softened
⅓ cup honey
1 large fresh pineapple, cored,
   peeled and cut into 1-inch
   cubes

3 fresh apricots, peaches or
   nectarines, cut into pieces
1 jar (4 ounces) maraschino
   cherries, drained

Combine butter and honey. Beginning and ending with pineapple, thread fruit pieces alternately on skewers. Brush kabobs with butter-honey mixture. Grill kabobs over medium-hot **Match light® charcoal briquets** 3 to 5 minutes or until fruit is heated through. Turn once or twice and brush with butter-honey mixture. Serve plain, with pound cake, ice cream or whipped topping, if desired.

Eggplant Parmesan

EGGPLANT PARMESAN

Makes 4 servings

1 eggplant (about 1¼ pounds)
½ cup olive or vegetable oil
½ teaspoon dried oregano
½ teaspoon dried rosemary
¼ teaspoon garlic powder

6 ounces sliced mozzarella or
    Monterey Jack cheese
1 cup freshly grated Parmesan
    cheese
1 jar (15 ounces) marinara sauce

Slice eggplant crosswise into ½-inch slices. Combine oil, oregano, rosemary
and garlic powder; mix well. Brush sides of eggplant with oil baste. Cut
mozzarella cheese into slices to fit eggplant slices; set aside. Grill eggplant,
on covered grill, over medium-hot **Kingsford® with Mesquite charcoal
briquets** 5 minutes, turning often and brushing with baste. Arrange cheese
slices on eggplant; spoon Parmesan cheese over each. Grill until cheeses
melt. Heat marinara sauce in small pan on edge of grill. Spoon hot sauce
over eggplant slices before serving.

HONEY MINT GRAPEFRUIT

Makes 4 to 6 servings

3 cups grapefruit segments, well
    drained (about 2 grapefruit)
⅓ cup honey

⅛ teaspoon mint flavoring
Mint sprigs, for garnish

Arrange grapefruit segments in lightly oiled foil pan. Drizzle honey and mint
flavoring over fruit. Cover pan tightly with foil. Place pan on grill over
medium-hot **Kingsford®** briquets 15 minutes or until fruit is hot. Garnish with
mint sprigs.

GRILLED APRICOTS AND PINEAPPLE

Makes 4 to 6 servings

1 can (20 ounces) pineapple
  chunks, drained
1 can (17 ounces) apricot halves,
  drained
1 tablespoon lemon juice

1 teaspoon grated lemon peel
2 tablespoons brown sugar
2 tablespoons butter or
  margarine

Arrange fruit in lightly oiled foil pan. Sprinkle lemon juice, peel and brown
sugar over fruit. Dot with butter. Cover pan tightly with foil. Place pan on grill
over medium-hot **Kingsford® briquets** 15 minutes or until fruit is hot.

CORN AU GRATIN

Makes 4 servings

1 can (17 ounces) whole kernel
  corn, drained*
¼ cup grated Cheddar cheese
2 tablespoons chopped green
  pepper

2 tablespoons finely chopped
  onion
½ teaspoon salt
⅛ teaspoon garlic powder
⅛ teaspoon pepper

Stir all ingredients together and spoon onto a large square of heavy-duty
foil. Fold foil loosely around corn and seal. Grill packet over medium-hot
Kingsford® briquets 15 minutes or until corn is hot. Turn packet once.

*You can substitute fresh corn-on-the-cob for canned corn. Cut 2 cups
whole corn from cob. No pre-cooking is necessary.

PEACHY COBBLER

Makes 8 servings

2 tablespoons butter or
  margarine
1 package (8 rolls) refrigerated
  caramel Danish rolls

1 can (21 ounces) peach pie
  filling

In 10-inch cast-iron skillet, combine butter and sugar-nut mixture from rolls.
Stir over medium heat until butter is melted. Place rolls in circle over butter-
sugar mixture. Spread pie filling over rolls. Cover skillet tightly with foil; place
on grill over medium-low **Kingsford® briquets** 10 to 15 minutes. Remove foil
and continue to grill 10 to 15 minutes longer or until rolls are cooked. Spoon
cobbler into dessert bowls; serve plain, with cream or ice cream, if desired.

POTATOES ROASTED IN COALS

Makes 6 servings

6 Washington Russet baking
    potatoes (about 10 ounces
    each)

Oil
Salsa (recipe follows)

Scrub potatoes; rub with oil. Pierce several times with fork. Individually wrap potatoes in oiled heavy-duty foil. Seal securely. Grill potatoes directly on hot **Kingsford®** briquets 1 hour or until tender, turning every 15 minutes. Remove potatoes from foil. Cut or pierce tops lengthwise; squeeze ends and push toward center to open. Spoon about 1/3 cup salsa into each potato. Top with sour cream, if desired.

SALSA

Makes 2 1/4 cups

1 1/2 cups chopped tomatoes
1/2 cup chopped onion
1/2 cup chopped cucumber
1/2 cup diced green chilies
1 tablespoon chopped green
    onion

1 tablespoon olive or vegetable
    oil
2 teaspoons lemon juice
3/4 teaspoon garlic salt
1/4 teaspoon dried oregano
Dash pepper

In medium bowl, combine all ingredients; mix well. (Recipe can be doubled.)
*Favorite recipe from **Alaska Seafood Marketing Institute, Salmon Division***

GRILLED STUFFED RED PEPPER RINGS

Makes 6 servings

4 medium red peppers
1 can (10 1/4 ounces) whole kernel
    corn, drained
1/2 cup dry bread crumbs
1 egg, beaten
1 tablespoon flour
2 tablespoons diced onion

2 tablespoons chopped parsley
1 1/2 cups prepared Hidden Valley
    Ranch® Original Ranch®
    Salad Dressing Mix
Salt and pepper
1 bunch fresh spinach, washed
    and trimmed

Cut 3 thick rings from each pepper; remove seeds. Arrange on oiled surface of large double-thick square of heavy-duty foil. Combine corn, bread crumbs, egg, flour, onion, parsley and 3/4 cup salad dressing; season with salt and pepper to taste. Spoon mixture into pepper rings and pack down. Fold foil over pepper rings to form tent; seal edges. Grill packet over medium-hot **Kingsford®** briquets about 15 minutes. Open foil tent to allow rings to cool. When ready to serve, line large serving plate with spinach leaves. With wide spatula, carefully transfer stuffed rings to lined plate. Serve with remaining salad dressing.

INDEX